# Getting to the Roots

# of Content-Area Vocabulary

rotation

independence

submarine

**Authors**

Timothy Rasinski, Ph.D.

Nancy Padak, Ed.D.

Rick M. Newton, Ph.D.

Evangeline Newton, Ph.D.

SHELL EDUCATION

## Publishing Credits

Robin Erickson, *Production Director*; Lee Aucoin, *Creative Director*;
Timothy J. Bradley, *Illustration Manager*; Sara Johnson, M.S.Ed., *Editorial Director*;
Jennifer Viñas, *Editor*; Grace Alba, *Designer*; Corinne Burton, M.A.Ed., *Publisher*

## Image Credits

p.29 whitemay/iStockphoto; All other images Shutterstock

## Standards

© 2004 Mid-continent Research for Education and Learning (McREL)
© 2010 National Governors Association Center for Best Practices and Council of Chief State School Officers (CCSS)

## Shell Education
5301 Oceanus Drive
Huntington Beach, CA  92649-1030
http://www.shelleducation.com
**ISBN 978-1-4258-0865-5**
© 2014 Shell Educational Publishing, Inc.

# Table of Contents

## Management

## Lessons

### Unit I—Social Studies Roots

# Table of Contents

# Content-Area Vocabulary Research and Practice

Content learning is largely conceptual. Words are labels for content-area concepts. Although learning these words is critical to student success, teaching them can be challenging. Asking students to look words up in their dictionaries or glossaries and then to memorize definitions provides, at best, a short-term solution. In this book, we present a systematic and research-based alternative to vocabulary learning: a roots approach. Because most words are defined (and spelled) by what their parts mean, students can expand their vocabularies by learning how words are built from the roots up. Over 90 percent of all academic vocabulary derives from Latin or Greek roots (prefixes, suffixes, bases). Moreover, when new academic words are added to English, they too are often derived from Latin and Greek roots. The logic goes like this: learning roots helps students learn content vocabulary; one root can help students unlock the meaning of multiple words. Knowing content vocabulary helps students comprehend and learn social studies, science, and mathematics.

> **Over 90 percent of all academic vocabulary derives from Latin or Greek roots.**

The units in this book center on common roots (prefixes and bases) in science, social studies, and mathematics. We present over 15 prefixes and bases that generate over 200 words from content-area vocabulary.

## What Does Research Say About Using a Roots Approach?

The size and depth of elementary students' vocabulary is associated with proficiency in reading comprehension. Effective vocabulary instruction results in higher levels of reading comprehension (Baumann et al. 2002; Beck, Perfetti, and McKeown 1982; Kame'enui, Carnine, and Freschi 1982; Stahl and Fairbanks 1986).

Morphological analysis (e.g., via a roots approach) is important because it is generative and allows students to make connections among semantically-related words or word families (Nagy and Scott 2000). In fact, developing morphological awareness is an integral component of word learning for young children (Biemiller and Slonim 2001). In a comprehensive review of 16 studies analyzing the effect of instruction in morphological awareness on literacy achievement, Carlisle (2010) observes that "children learn morphemes as they learn language" (465).

Classroom-based studies have demonstrated the effectiveness of teaching word parts and context clues in the primary and intermediate grades (Baumann et al. 2005; Biemiller 2005; Mountain 2005; Porter-Collier 2010; Baumann et al. 2002; Carlisle 2000; Kieffer and Lesaux 2007). Research in content-area vocabulary has demonstrated the effectiveness of teaching Greek and Latin word roots, especially for struggling readers (Harmon et al. 2005).

# Content-Area Vocabulary Research and Practice *(cont.)*

No single instructional method is sufficient. Teachers need a variety of methods that teach word meanings while also increasing the depth of word knowledge (Blachowicz et al. 2006; Lehr, Osborn, and Hiebert 2004). These methods should aim at fostering:

### Immersion

Students need frequent opportunities to use new words in diverse oral and print contexts in order to learn them thoroughly (Blachowicz and Fisher 2006).

### Metacognitive and metalinguistic awareness

Students must understand and know how to manipulate the structural features of language (Nagy and Scott 2000).

### Word consciousness

Word exploration (e.g., etymology) and word play (e.g., puns, riddles, games) help students develop an awareness of and interest in words (Graves and Watts-Taffe 2002, Lehr et al. 2004).

# Content-Area Vocabulary Research and Practice (cont.)

## What Is a Root?

A *root* is a word part that contains meaning and not merely sound. Roots are vocabulary multipliers—each root taught helps students discover the meanings of multiple words. There are three categories of roots, depending on their placement within a word:

### prefix

A root at the beginning of a word. For example, in the word *retraction*, the initial *re-* is a prefix, meaning "back," "again."

### base

The core root, which provides a word with its basic meaning. In the word *retraction*, the base is *tract*, which means "pull," "draw," "drag."

### suffix

A root that ends a word. In the word *retraction*, the final *-ion* is a suffix, meaning "act of," "state of."

**Note:** The term *affix*, used in the Common Core State Standards, refers to either prefixes or suffixes. *Affix* contains an assimilated form of the prefix *ad-*, which means "to," "toward," or "add to." And the Latin base *fix-* means "fasten" or "stick." So an *affix* is a part of a word "added or fixed to" a base word either in front (prefix) or at the end (suffix).

## What Do Prefixes and Suffixes Do?

A prefix serves one of three functions:

* A prefix can *negate* a word by meaning "not." The most common negating prefixes are *un-* (e.g., *unhappy, unwashed*) and negative *in-, im-, il-* (e.g., *invisible, impossible, illegal*). Some directional prefixes can also be negating. For example, the prefix variations *di-, dis-, dif-*, which mean "apart," "in different directions," can also mean "not" (*dis*similar = "not similar," a *dif*ficult task is "not" easy).

* A prefix can be *directional*: it sends the base of a word in a specific direction. The prefix *ex-* means "out," *re-* means "back," "again," *sub-* means "under," "below," and *ad-* means "to," "toward," "add to." For example, an *ex*it sign indicates the way "out" of a building; we *de*scend a staircase when we go "down"; when class *con*venes, it comes "together"; when class is *dis*missed, students scatter "in different directions"; when they *pro*ceed to their buses, they move "forward," "ahead" to their bus stops.

* A prefix can have *intensifying force*, meaning "very," "thoroughly." A *per*fectly baked cake, for example, is "thoroughly" done. Quantitative and numerical prefixes are also intensifying.

A suffix changes the part of speech (e.g., *act, action; swift, swiftly*) or modifies the base (e.g., *fast, faster*).

# Content-Area Vocabulary Research and Practice (cont.)

## What Is Assimilation?

Some prefixes have multiple forms because of an easily recognizable and predictable phenomenon called *assimilation*. Assimilation simply means that some consonants at the beginning of a word change and become like ("similar to" = assimilate) the consonants that follow them. For example, the prefix *con-* occurs in the words *convention* and *conference*. Through assimilation, it also appears in *collect*, *commotion*, and *correct*. The reason is simple: assimilation makes a word easier to pronounce (consider *conlect* vs. *collect*). Although assimilation causes spelling changes, the meaning of the prefix does not change.

While this concept does not apply to every lesson in this book, as your students become more "roots" aware, they may raise questions about why the spelling of some prefixes changes. The following information will help answer these questions.

## Latin Prefixes that Assimilate

| Prefix | Meaning | Examples |
| --- | --- | --- |
| *ad-* | to, toward, add to | *admit, accelerate, affect, aggravate, allusion, appendix, arrogant, assimilate, attract* |
| *con-, co-* | with, together, very | *congregate, coworker, collect, combine, commit, compose, correct* |
| *ex-, e-, ef-* | out, from, completely | *expose, edict, effect* |
| *dis-, di-, dif-* | apart, in different directions, not | *disintegrate, divert, different, difficult* |
| *in-, im-, il-* (directional) | in, on, into, against | *induct, insert, imbibe, immigrant, import, impose, illustrate* |
| *in-, im-, il-* (negative) | not | *infinite, insatiable, ignoble, illegal, illegible, impossible, irresponsible* |
| *ob-* | toward, up against | *obstruct, occurrence, offensive, oppose* |
| *sub-* | under, up from under | *submarine, succeed, suffer, support, suspend* |

# Content-Area Vocabulary Research and Practice (cont.)

## Types of Assimilation

### Unassimilated Prefixes

We can easily pronounce the unaltered prefix with the base. Hence, there is no need to assimilate.

con + vention = convention       ob + struction = obstruction

in + visible = invisible       ex + pose = expose

sub + terranean = subterranean       dis + tract = distract

### Partial Assimilation

We cannot easily pronounce *n* when it is followed by such consonants as *b, p,* and (occasionally) *f.* In such cases, the final *n* of the prefix partially assimilates into *m.*

in + possible = impossible       con + bine = combine

con + pose = compose       con + fort = comfort

### Full Assimilation

We cannot easily pronounce these unaltered prefixes when followed by certain consonants. In such cases, the final consonant of the prefix changes into the initial consonant of the base that follows it. The result is a doubled consonant near the beginning.

con + rect = correct       ex + fect = effect

in + legal = illegal       dis + fer = differ

sub + fer = suffer       ad + similation = assimilation

ob + pose = oppose

# Content-Area Vocabulary Research and Practice *(cont.)*

## Why Teach with a Roots Approach?

Teaching with a roots approach is efficient. Over 60 percent of the words students encounter in their reading have recognizable word parts (Nagy et al. 1989). Moreover, content-area vocabulary is largely of Greek and Latin origin (Harmon, Hedrick, and Wood 2005). Many words from Greek and Latin roots meet the criteria for "tier two" words and are appropriate for instruction (Beck, McKeown, and Kucan 2002).

Root study promotes independent word learning, even in the primary grades (Carlisle 2010). In addition, roots are word multipliers— that is, knowledge of one root can help students determine the meaning, pronunciation, and spelling of 10, 20, or more English words. With roots, students learn to make

> **Latin and Greek word roots follow linguistic patterns that can help students with the meaning, sound, and spelling of English words.**

connections among words that are semantically related (Nagy and Scott 2000). Research suggests that the brain is a pattern detector (Cunningham 2004). Latin and Greek word roots follow linguistic patterns that can help students with the meaning, sound, and spelling of English words. Indeed, Latin and Greek roots have consistent orthographic (spelling) patterns (Rasinski and Padak 2013; Bear et al. 2011).

Young readers' word instruction is often characterized by a study of word patterns called *rimes, phonograms,* or *word families.* A Latin-Greek roots approach is the next logical and developmental step in word learning (Bear et al. 2011). Many English language learners speak first languages semantically related to Latin. For example, more than 75 percent of the words in Spanish come from Latin (Chandler and Schwartz 1961/1991). In fact, Spanish, Portuguese, French, Catalan, Italian, and Rumanian are all classified as "Romance Languages" because they derive from Latin, the language of ancient Romans. Enhancing this natural linguistic connection inherent in many of these languages can accelerate these students' vocabulary growth (Blachowicz et al. 2006).

Many states are beginning to include a study of roots, including Latin and Greek derivations, in their elementary and middle school literacy standards. Indeed, the Common Core State Standards focus extensively on root-specific standards in the "Reading Foundational Skills" and "Language/Vocabulary Acquisition and Use" sections. According to these standards, attention to roots should begin in kindergarten.

# Content-Area Vocabulary Research and Practice (cont.)

## Differentiating Instruction

Some students, such as struggling readers or those learning English, may need additional support. Others may benefit from additional challenge. These ideas may help you differentiate instruction:

- Use visual aids.

- Ask students to sketch or act out words. Others can guess the depicted words.

- Reduce length of activity.

- Pair students. Encourage them to talk about the roots and the activities.

- Challenge students to create new words that contain the root. Others can guess what the made-up words mean.

- Talk students through the necessary process to complete an activity. Your aim should be to scaffold students' thinking, not to provide answers.

- As we point out in individual lesson descriptions, encourage talk.

- Have students keep a personal vocabulary journal in which they list the roots and related words they learn. Encourage students to use their new vocabulary in their oral and written language (e.g., "use at least one word containing the *tract* root in your journal entry today").

- Put the roots and words derived from the roots on display in the classroom. Keep them on display over the course of several weeks. (You may wish to move some of the displays into the hallway or other sites outside your classroom.)

- Play word games that involve the roots with your students often. Appendix E (pages 149–156) provides lists of words containing the roots used in this book.

Students who need additional challenge can a) look for words containing the featured root in their content-area texts, b) write riddles for others to solve using several words that contain the root, or c) use an online resource to find additional words containing the root (e.g., http://onelook.com) or to create word puzzles featuring the root (e.g., http://puzzlemaker.com).

Like their peers, English language learners benefit from the focus on meaning using research-based strategies to learn new roots and words. Especially if students' native languages derive from Latin (e.g., Spanish), make comparisons to the native languages whenever possible. (You can look online for resources to assist with this.) When Spanish speakers learn to look for roots within words, they will be able to relate many word roots in English to their counterparts in Spanish. Sharing their knowledge with other classmates will help everyone grow.

# How to Use This Book

This book offers three units. Unit I presents two prefixes, two bases, and one suffix for words that appear in social studies. Unit II presents five bases for words that appear in science. Unit III presents two numerical prefixes and three bases for words that appear in mathematics. The following information will help you implement each lesson within the three units.

## Lesson Overview

A list of **Standards** (McREL and Common Core State Standards) is included in each lesson.

The **Materials** listed include the activity pages for students.

**Teaching Tips** provide essential information about the root. Reading this section before you teach the lesson will provide you with a foundation to ensure student success.

The **Guided Practice** portion of each lesson includes suggestions for implementing each of the student activity pages.

The **About the Root** activities are introductions and include short passages using the root of focus. The purpose of these passages is to show students contextual use of the root in the content areas. As students read to themselves or listen to the teacher read aloud, they identify the prefix or suffix words in extended texts that center on a wide range of interesting topics.

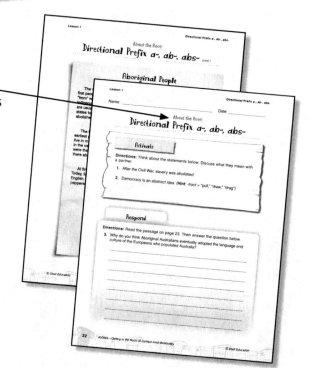

# How to Use This Book (cont.)

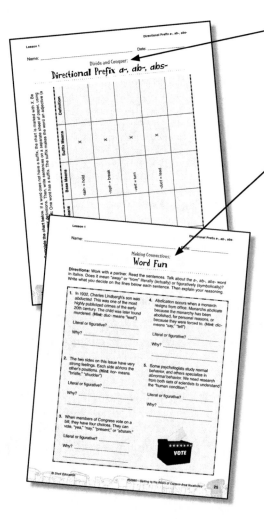

The **Divide and Conquer** activities allow students to pull words apart. They dissect the parts of the words, understand the meaning of these parts, and then gain a greater understanding of the word as a whole.

The **Making Connections** activities allow students to use their knowledge of roots to make connections to vocabulary and offer students the opportunity to extend their exploration of the root(s) through activities such as word sorts, riddles, representing the roots and related words in drawings, and gamelike tasks. They may need to distinguish when to use a certain root or which way the root is used in a word.

All of the student activity pages and additional resources can be found on the **Digital Resource CD**.

# How to Use This Book (cont.)

## Tips for Implementation

As you think about how you will teach the lessons, refer to the tips below on how to implement each one.

* You can teach the lessons in any order. You may want to coordinate with your curriculum and with your grade-level colleagues.

* Each lesson cycle addresses one root.

* Before beginning a new lesson, read the brief teaching tips and guided practice.

* Talking about the roots is very important for student learning. This approach to vocabulary development goes far beyond mere memorization of specific words (which, according to research, does not work). Students need to learn to think about how roots contribute to meanings. Talking this through can help them develop this realization. So, encourage students to talk, Talk, TALK!!! You will notice that the teacher directions for every Divide and Conquer activity include a brief etymological explanation of all words in the Divide and Conquer list. These explanations will help you guide the in-class discussion. These conversations, which need only take a few minutes, should focus on helping students think deeply about root meanings. For examples of etymological breakdown of the words, see the Answer Key (pages 116–123)

**Note:** We have suggested discussion questions and included answers for all of the Divide and Conquer activities. The answers are for your use only. They may help you lead discussions and conversations about how the roots contribute to meaning.

* Your direct involvement is needed for the Divide and Conquer activities. This is the process students use to determine meaning. They learn to look for meaningful chunks of words ("divide") and to use this information to "conquer" the meaning of the longer word. To help students see the logic inherent in divide and conquer, you can make an analogy to addition (*transport* = *trans* [across] + *port* [carry] = carry across) or "if/then" statements: If *trans* means "across" and *port* means "carry," then *transport* means "to carry something across an area." Be certain that students say the meaning of the longer word in a way that makes sense: "carry across," not "across carry." After students have divided and conquered, help them see how the roots "add up to" the meaning of the words.

* Students can complete the About the Root and Making Connections activities independently, in pairs, or as homework.

* Each week, display the root(s) and meaning(s) prominently in your classroom.

# How to Use This Book (cont.)

- Encourage students to use the root of the week as much as possible. Reading, writing, speaking, and listening to words containing the root will facilitate learning. Several generic activities are suggested in Appendix C (pages 126–128) to provide additional instruction or practice, if you or your students wish.

## Introducing Each Lesson

Introduce each root by linking to words that students already know. Ideas are provided in the Teaching Tips sections. In addition, you could:

- Put two or three common words containing the root on the board and ask students to talk about what meaning they share. You may want to embed these in phrases.

- Tell students, "The root of the week is _____. It means _____." Ask them to work with partners to generate words containing the root. Make a class list, and discuss common meaning.

- Encourage students to use the root's definition in their talk about words containing the root.

## Assessment

At least one part of each lesson could be used for assessment purposes. In addition, you will find matching exercises that are also suitable for assessment in Appendix D (pages 132–148) or on the Digital Resource CD (filename: additionalassessments.pdf). You can use a simple three-point scale to record students' performances: Outstanding, Satisfactory, or Unsatisfactory. Informal assessment techniques can supplement this information:

- Use a knowledge-rating chart with students. To do this, select key words from something students will read. Make a three-column chart for students to indicate if they a) know a word well, b) have seen or heard it, or c) don't know it at all.

- Have students keep word journals in which they a) record information about roots and the words that contain them or b) keep lists of interesting words from their reading. Ask students to peruse their journals occasionally to draw some conclusions about their word knowledge.

- Encourage students to use self-assessment. Ask them to write about a) their own word knowledge, b) where they find new and interesting words, and/or c) what strategies they use most often to figure out the meaning of new words.

# Correlation to the Standards

Shell Education is committed to producing educational materials that are research and standards based. In this effort, we have correlated all of our products to the academic standards of all 50 United States, the District of Columbia, the Department of Defense Dependent Schools, and all Canadian provinces.

## How To Find Standards Correlations

To print a customized correlation report of this product for your state, visit our website at http://www.shelleducation.com and follow the on-screen directions. If you require assistance in printing correlation reports, please contact Customer Service at 1-877-777-3450.

## Purpose and Intent of Standards

Legislation mandates that all states adopt academic standards that identify the skills students will learn in kindergarten through grade twelve. Many states also have standards for Pre–K. This same legislation sets requirements to ensure the standards are detailed and comprehensive.

Standards are designed to focus instruction and guide adoption of curricula. Standards are statements that describe the criteria necessary for students to meet specific academic goals. They define the knowledge, skills, and content students should acquire at each level. Standards are also used to develop standardized tests to evaluate students' academic progress. Teachers are required to demonstrate how their lessons meet state standards. State standards are used in the development of all of our products, so educators can be assured they meet the academic requirements of each state.

## Common Core State Standards

Many lessons in this book are aligned to the Common Core State Standards (CCSS). The standards support the objectives presented throughout the lessons and are provided on the Digital Resource CD (standards.pdf).

## McREL Compendium

We use the Mid-continent Research for Education and Learning (McREL) Compendium to create standards correlations. Each year, McREL analyzes state standards and revises the compendium. By following this procedure, McREL is able to produce a general compilation of national standards. Each lesson in this product is based on one or more McREL standards, which are provided on the Digital Resource CD (standards.pdf).

## TESOL and WIDA Standards

The lessons in this book promote English language development for English language learners. The standards listed on the Digital Resource CD (standards.pdf) support the language objectives presented throughout the lessons.

# Standards Chart

| McREL Standard | Page(s) |
|---|---|
| **Language Arts 5.4**—Uses phonetic and structural analysis techniques, syntactic structure, and semantic context to decode unknown words. | All Lessons |
| **Language Arts 5.4**—Uses a variety of context clues to decode unknown words. | All Lessons |
| **Common Core State Standard** | **Page(s)** |
| **Literacy RI.5.4**—Determine the meaning of general academic and domain-specific words and phrases in a text relevant to a grade 5 topic or subject area. | All Lessons |
| **Literacy RF.5.3.a**—Use combined knowledge of all letter-sound correspondences, syllabication patterns, and morphology to read accurately unfamiliar multisyllabic words in context and out of context. | All Lessons |
| **Literacy L.5.4.b**—Use common, grade-appropriate Greek and Latin affixes and roots as clues to the meaning of a word. | All Lessons |
| **Speaking and Listening 5.1.d**—Review the key ideas expressed and draw conclusions in light of information and knowledge gained from the discussions. | All Lessons |
| **TESOL and WIDA Standard** | **Page(s)** |
| English language learners **communicate** for **social**, **intercultural**, and **instructional** purposes within the school setting. | All Lessons |
| English language learners **communicate** information, ideas, and concepts necessary for academic success in the area of **language arts**. | All Lessons |

# About the Authors

**Timothy Rasinski, Ph.D.**, is a professor of literacy education at Kent State University. He has written over 150 articles and has authored, coauthored, or edited over 15 books and curriculum programs on reading education. His research on reading has been cited by the National Reading Panel and has been published in journals such as *Reading Research Quarterly, The Reading Teacher, Reading Psychology*, and *The Journal of Educational Research*. Tim served on the Board of Directors of the International Reading Association, and from 1992–1999, he was coeditor of *The Reading Teacher*, the world's most widely read journal of literacy education. He has also served as editor of the *Journal of Literacy Research*, one of the premier research journals in reading. Tim is a past president of the College Reading Association, and he has won the A.B. Herr Award from the College Reading Association for his scholarly contributions to literacy education. In 2010, Tim was elected into the International Reading Hall of Fame.

**Nancy Padak, Ed.D.**, is an active researcher, author, and consultant. She was a Distinguished Professor in the College and Graduate School of Education, Health, and Human Services at Kent State University. She directed KSU's Reading and Writing Center and taught in the area of literacy education. She was the Principal Investigator for the Ohio Literacy Resource Center, which has provided support for adult and family literacy programs since 1993. Prior to her arrival at Kent State in 1985, she was a classroom teacher and district administrator. She has written or edited more than 25 books and more than 90 chapters and articles. She has also served in a variety of leadership roles in professional organizations, including the presidency of the College Reading Association and (with others) the Editor of *The Reading Teacher* and the *Journal of Literacy Research*. She has won several awards for her scholarship and contributions to literacy education.

# About the Authors *(cont.)*

**Rick M. Newton, Ph.D.**, holds a doctoral degree in Greek and Latin from the University of Michigan and is now an emeritus professor of Greek and Latin at Kent State University. He developed the course "English Words from Classical Elements," which more than 15,000 Kent State students have taken over the past 30 years. He holds the Distinguished Teaching Award from the Kent State College of Arts and Sciences and the Translation Award from the Modern Greek Studies Association of North America and Canada.

**Evangeline Newton, Ph.D.**, is a professor of literacy education at the University of Akron, where she served as the first director of the Center for Literacy. She teaches a variety of literacy methods courses and professional development workshops to elementary, middle, and high school teachers. A former coeditor of *The Ohio Reading Teacher*, Evangeline currently chairs the Reading Review Board of the Ohio Resource Center for Mathematics, Science, and Reading. She serves on editorial review boards for *The Reading Teacher* and *Reading Horizons*. Evangeline is active in the Association of Literacy Educators and the International Reading Association (IRA). As a participant in IRA's Reading and Writing for Critical Thinking project, Evangeline taught workshops for teachers and Peace Corps volunteers in Armenia. A former St. Louis public school teacher, Evangeline holds a B.A. from Washington University in St. Louis, an M.A.T. from Webster University, and a Ph.D. from Kent State University.

# Directional Prefix *a-, ab-, abs-*

## *a-, ab-,* and *abs-* = "away," "from"

## Standards

Uses phonetic and structural analysis techniques, syntactic structure, and semantic context to decode unknown words

Determines the meaning of general academic and domain-specific words and phrases in a text relevant to a grade 5 topic or subject area

Reviews the key ideas expressed and draws conclusions in light of information and knowledge gained from the discussions

## Materials

- *About the Root: Directional Prefix* a-, ab-, abs- (pages 22–23)

- *Divide and Conquer: Directional Prefix* a-, ab-, abs- (page 24)

- *Making Connections: Word Fun* (page 25)

## Teaching Tips

- The directional prefix *a-, ab-, abs-* means "away" or "from." This prefix appears in words describing literal and physical separation. For example, *abduct*—to lead someone "away from" the premises; *absent*—being physically "away from" class. It also appears in words describing figurative separation (e.g., *abstain*—to hold one's vote "away from" an election).

- The three forms of this prefix (*a-, ab-, abs-*) have the same meaning. The particular form used in a word is determined by the first letter of the base to which it attaches. Students do not need to differentiate between whether *a-, ab-, abs-* mean "away" or "from" in each of the individual words they work with. The goal is for them to associate all *a-, ab-, abs-* words with the general idea of separation.

## Guided Practice

### About the Root: Directional Prefix *a-, ab-, abs-*

1. Write *absent* on the board. Ask students to discuss with neighbors what it means. Invite sharing. Tell students that the base *-ent* means "being" or "to be." Ask students to discuss with neighbors what the prefix *abs-* means. Invite sharing, and tell students that *a-, ab-, abs-* means "away" or "from." Ask students to help you fill in these blanks: If *abs-* means _____ and *-ent* means _____, then *absent* means _____ (away; be; being away).

# Directional Prefix a-, ab-, abs- (cont.)

**2.** Write the words *literal* and *figurative* on the board. Ask students to talk with neighbors about the difference in these two types of meanings. Explain that words with *a-, ab-, abs-* may have literal (actual) or figurative (not actual) meanings of "away" or "from." Ask partners to decide whether the words *absent* and *abrupt* show literal or figurative "from" or "away." Invite students to share their thinking.

**3.** Ask students to complete the About the Root pages. They can work individually or with partners. After they have finished, invite whole-group conversation. Students can share answers, talk about the text passage, or generate more words containing the root.

**4.** After students have discussed the Activate activity, invite whole-group conversation. You may wish to have students write down the shared ideas to revisit at a later time.

## Divide and Conquer: Directional Prefix a-, ab-, abs-

**5.** As you guide students through Divide and Conquer, use the questions below to generate discussion about each of the words:

- Where is the meaning of "away" or "from" in the word _____? Is it a literal or a figurative "away" or "from"?

- Where might you see the word _____?

- Can you think of an example of _____?

- Does _____ have more than one meaning? If so, how are those meanings the same? How are they different?

- How is the word _____ different from the word _____?

- What other words meaning "away" or "from" do you know that contain the prefix *a-, ab-, abs-*?

- Does the word have a suffix? (Students respond.) If yes, what does the suffix do? Can you think of other words that have this suffix?

## Making Connections: Word Fun

**6.** Invite students to share reasons for deciding if a word has a literal or a figurative use. Focus conversation on helping students understand the concepts *literal* and *figurative*.

### Words with a-, ab-, abs-

| | |
|---|---|
| abandon | abrogate |
| abate | abrupt |
| abdicate | abscond |
| abduct | absent |
| abeyance | absolve |
| abhorrent | absorb |
| abject | abstain |
| abolish | abstract |
| abort | abuse |
| abrade | |

To print a full list of words for students, see page 149.

Name: _____    Date: _____

## About the Root:
# Directional Prefix *a-, ab-, abs-*

### Activate

**Directions:** Think about the statements below. Discuss what they mean with a partner.

1. After the Civil War, slavery was *abolished*.

2. Democracy is an *abstract* idea. (**Hint**: *-tract* = "pull," "draw," "drag")

### Respond

**Directions:** Read the passage on page 23. Then answer the question below.

3. Why do you think Aboriginal Australians eventually adopted the language and culture of the Europeans who populated Australia?

_____

_____

_____

_____

_____

_____

_____

# Directional Prefix *a-, ab-, abs-* (cont.)

## Aboriginal People

The word *aboriginal* refers to a country's original inhabitants who are the first people to live in or come "from" that land. They live on the same land "from" which their people "originated." Aboriginal people are sometimes called indigenous people (the word *indigenous* means "born within" a region). They are usually groups of ethnic minorities who were disregarded or ignored as states took over their lands. Sometimes, aboriginal people's cultures were even abolished as new people settled in their areas.

The term *aborigine* (ab-uh-RIJ-uh-nee) was first used to describe the earliest people to live in Greece and Italy. Today, colonies of aboriginal people live in many places around the world. For example, many aboriginal people live in the vast and largely unexplored continent of Australia. Aboriginal Australians were the first human beings to come to the continent of Australia. They migrated there about 50,000 years ago.

At first, these indigenous people had their own languages and culture. Today, for the most part, they have adopted Australian culture and speak English. However, they have not abandoned their roots. Their English is peppered with Aboriginal words and phrases.

Name: _____     Date: _____

## Divide and Conquer:
# Directional Prefix a-, ab-, abs-

**Directions:** Complete the chart below. If a word does not have a suffix, the chart is marked with X. Be sure to use *away* or *from* in your definitions. Then, write sentences on a separate sheet of paper, using two of the words from the chart. **Hint:** One word has a suffix. The suffix makes the word an adjective (a describing word).

| Word | Prefix Means | Base Means | Suffix Means | Definition |
|------|--------------|------------|--------------|------------|
| 1. abstain | | -*tain*- = hold | X | |
| 2. abrupt | | -*rupt*- = break | X | |
| 3. avert | | -*vert* = turn | X | |
| 4. abduct | | -*duct* = lead | X | |
| 5. abnormal | | | | |

Name: _____  Date: _____

## Making Connections:
# Word Fun

· · · · · · · · · · · · · · · · · · · · · · · · · · · · · · · · · · · · · · · · · · · ·

**Directions:** Work with a partner. Read the sentences. Talk about the *a-, ab-, abs-* word in italics. Does it mean "away" or "from" literally (actually) or figuratively (symbolically)? Write what you decide on the lines below each sentence. Then explain your reasoning.

1. In 1932, Charles Lindbergh's son was *abducted*. This was one of the most highly publicized crimes of the early 20th century. The child was later found murdered. (**Hint:** *duc-* means "lead")

   Literal or figurative? _____

   Why? _____

   _____

2. The two sides on this issue have very strong feelings. Each side *abhors* the other's positions. (**Hint:** *hor-* means "bristle," "shudder")

   Literal or figurative? _____

   Why? _____

   _____

3. When members of Congress vote on a bill, they have four choices. They can vote, "yea," "nay," "present," or "*abstain*."

   Literal or figurative? _____

   Why? _____

   _____

4. *Abdication* occurs when a monarch resigns from office. Monarchs *abdicate* because the monarchy has been abolished, for personal reasons, or because they were forced to. (**Hint:** *dic-* means "say," "tell")

   Literal or figurative? _____

   Why? _____

   _____

5. Some psychologists study normal behavior, and others specialize in *abnormal* behavior. We need research from both sets of scientists to understand the "human condition."

   Literal or figurative? _____

   Why? _____

   _____

# Directional Prefix ad-

## ad- = "to," "toward," "add to"

## Standards

Uses a variety of context clues to decode unknown words

Uses combined knowledge of all letter-sound correspondences, syllabication patterns, and morphology to read accurately unfamiliar multisyllabic words in context and out of context

Reviews the key ideas expressed and draws conclusions in light of information and knowledge gained from the discussions

## Materials

- *About the Root: Directional Prefix* ad- (pages 28–29)

- *Divide and Conquer: Directional Prefix* ad- (page 30)

- *Making Connections: Word Sort* (page 31)

## Teaching Tips

- The Latin directional prefix *ad-*, meaning "to," "toward," or "add to," is found in many English words. Students may already know words beginning with this prefix. For example, when we perform *addition,* we "add" one number "to" another. The purpose of an *advertisement* is to draw our attention "to" or "toward" a product.

- This prefix appears in words describing literal and physical clinging "to" something (e.g., *adhesive* tape *adheres* "to" the surface with *adhesion*). It also appears in words describing figurative clinging "to" something (e.g., we *adhere* to a diet by "sticking to" it; we *adhere* to our beliefs when we "cling to" them).

- The prefix *ad-* frequently undergoes the process of assimilation by changing its final *d* into the same consonant as the base to which it attaches: *ad-* + *fect* = *affect; ad-* + *tract* = *attract; ad-* + *celerate* = *accelerate.* This lesson only presents *ad-* words that have not assimilated. (For more on assimilation, see pages 8–9.)

- Students do not need to differentiate between whether *ad-* means "to," "toward," or "add to" in each of the individual words they work with. The goal is for them to associate all *ad-* words with the general idea of addition or motion toward.

## Guided Practice

### About the Root: Directional Prefix ad-

1. Write the prefix *ad-* on the board. Directly under it, write the sentences *The United States and Canada are adjacent countries* and *All citizens must adhere to the laws of the land.*

# Directional Prefix ad- (cont.)

**2.** Explain that the base *jac-* means "to lie" and the base *her-* means "to stick or cling." Ask partners to figure out the meaning of the prefix *ad-*. Invite sharing. Stress that *ad-* means "to," "toward," or "add to."

**3.** Ask students to complete the About the Root pages. They can work individually or with partners. After they have finished, invite whole-group conversation. Students can share answers, talk about the text passage, or generate more words containing the root.

**4.** After students have discussed the Activate activity, invite whole-group conversation. You may wish to have students write down the shared ideas to revisit at a later time.

## Divide and Conquer: Directional Prefix ad-

**5.** As you guide students through Divide and Conquer, use questions like these to generate discussion about each of the words:

- Where is the meaning of "to," "toward," or "add to" in the word _____?

- Where might you see the word _____?

- Can you think of an example of _____?

- Does _____ have more than one meaning? If so, how are those meanings the same? How are they different?

- How is the word _____ different from the word _____?

- Do you know any other words that begin with *ad-*? How do these words contain the meaning of "to," "toward," or "add to"?

- Does the word have a suffix? (Students respond.) If yes, what does the suffix do? Can you think of other words that have this suffix?

## Making Connections: Word Sort

**6.** Conclude with conversation. The syllable sort choices are either right or wrong, but the "is or could describe a person" sort invites more divergent responses. Ask students to explain their reasoning for their choices.

### Words with ad-

| | |
|---|---|
| adapt | admire |
| adaptive | admission |
| add | admit |
| addendum | admittedly |
| addition | admonition |
| additional | adorn |
| additive | advance |
| address | advancement |
| adduce | advantage |
| adhere | adventure |
| adherence | adventurer |
| adhesion | adventuresome |
| adhesive | adverb |
| adjacent | adverse |
| adjective | advertise |
| adjoin | advertisement |
| adjunct | advice |
| admiration | |

To print a full list of words for students, see page 149.

Name: _____   Date: _____

**About the Root:**
# Directional Prefix ad-

## Activate

**Directions:** Think about how each italicized word means "to," "toward," or "add to" in the sentences below. Discuss them with a partner.

1. With the *addition* of Alaska and Hawaii in 1959, the United States now has 50 states.

2. In 1990, The Americans with Disabilities Act became law. This law requires reasonable *adaptations* in public buildings, such as wheelchair ramps, for persons with physical disabilities. (**Hint**: *-apt-* means "join" or "fitted.")

## Respond

**Directions:** Read the passage on page 29. Then answer the questions below.

3. Which man had the advantage in the Hamilton/Burr duel? Why?

_____

_____

_____

4. Whom do you think history has treated more harshly? Why do you think so?

_____

_____

_____

## About the Root:
# Directional Prefix ad- (cont.)

## Famous Adversaries—
## Alexander Hamilton and Aaron Burr

American history is full of *adversarial* relationships. Indeed, each election has at least two people who are *adversaries* (*vers-* = "turn"), candidates who "turn" "toward" each other in disagreement and rivalry. However, some *adversarial* situations are more serious than others. In fact, a famous one, between Alexander Hamilton and Aaron Burr, ended in death. Here's the story:

The date and place: July 11, 1804, Weehawken, New Jersey. The characters: Alexander Hamilton, a Founding Father, who was the nation's first secretary of the treasury and Aaron Burr, Thomas Jefferson's vice president. The men had been fighting a "war of words" for years. They disagreed politically, *admonished* one another often, and had several loud and public skirmishes about specific political events.

Hamilton made an address in which he spoke critically of Burr. When Burr found out, he challenged Hamilton to a duel. Several people tried to dissuade the men, but the men would not take others' *advice*. The duel went forth. Each man fired one shot from a dueling pistol. Hamilton was mortally wounded; he died the next day. Burr was charged with murder.

Name: _____     Date: _____

## Divide and Conquer:
# Directional Prefix ad-

**Directions:** Complete the chart below. If a word does not have a suffix, the chart is marked with X. Be sure to use *to*, *toward*, or *add to* in your definitions. Then, write sentences on a separate sheet of paper, using two of the words from the chart. **Hint:** Two words have suffixes. In one case, the suffix makes the word a noun (a person). In the other, the suffix makes the word a verb (an action word).

| Word | Prefix Means | Base Means | Suffix Means | Definition |
|------|--------------|------------|--------------|------------|
| 1. adapt | | -*apt* = fit | X | |
| 2. admonish | | -*mon*- = warn | | |
| 3. adhere | | -*her* = stick, cling | X | |
| 4. advent | | -*vent* = come | X | |
| 5. adversary | | -*vers*- = turn | | |

Name: Divine      Date: I don't care!!!

## Making Connections:
# Word Sort

**Directions:** Use the words in the Word Bank to complete the chart below. Explain your thinking to a partner.

**Word Bank**

adapt    additional    adhesion    advent
adaptive    address    adjective    adversary
addendum    adhere    admonish

| 2 Syllables | 3 Syllables | 4 or More Syllables |
|---|---|---|
| adapt | adaptive | additional |
| address | addendum | adversary |
| adhere | adhesion | |
| advent | admonish | |
| | adjective | |

| Is or Could Describe a Person | Is Not/Could Not Describe a Person | |
|---|---|---|
| adapt  adaptive | addendum | adhesion |
| additional | advent | adjective |
| adversary | admonish | adress |
| adaptive | adhere | |

| Describes An Action | Does Not Describe An Action | |
|---|---|---|
| adapt | admonish | addendum |
| advent | adversary | adhesion |
| adhere | additional | adjective |
| adress | adaptive | |

# Base sed-, sid-, sess-

## sed-, sid-, sess- = "sit," "settle"

## Standards

Uses phonetic and structural analysis techniques, syntactic structure, and semantic context to decode unknown words

Uses common, grade-appropriate Greek and Latin affixes (a word part added or fixed to a base or root word) and roots as clues to the meaning of a word

Reviews the key ideas expressed and draws conclusions in light of information and knowledge gained from the discussions

## Materials

- *About the Root: Base* sed-, sid-, sess- (pages 34–35)

- *Divide and Conquer: Base* sed-, sid-, sess- (page 36)

- *Making Connections: Magic Square* (page 37)

## Teaching Tips

- The Latin base *sed-, sid-, sess-* means "sit" or "settle." Students may already know words beginning with this base, although they may not associate these words with "sitting" or "settling." For example, when class is in *session,* students are "sitting" at their desks. *Sediment* consists of the silt and gravel that "settles" or "sits" at the bottom of a river. A person who *presides* over a meeting "sits" at the head of the table.

- This base can describe the literal and physical state of "sitting" or "settling." For example, we sit at *sedentary* jobs. *Sedimentary* rocks consist of compacted physical *residue*. This base can also describe figurative "settling." People take *sedatives* to "settle" or calm their nerves. When political tensions *subside,* things tend to "settle" down.

- The form *sed-* usually appears in words without prefixes (e.g., *sediment, sedentary, sedate, sedative, sedation*). The form *sid-* appears in words with prefixes (e.g., *subside, reside, residue, resident, president*).

## Guided Practice

### About the Root: Base sed-, sid-, sess-

1. Write *sed-, sid-, sess-* on the board. Tell students that this base means "sit" or "settle." Write the phrases *class session, residue from a storm, sitting presidents,* and *urban resident* on the board. Ask partners to determine where the "sit" or "settle" is in each phrase. After a few minutes, invite sharing.

# Base sed-, sid-, sess- (cont.)

**2.** Ask students to complete the About the Root pages. They can work individually or with partners. After they have finished, invite whole-group conversation. Students can share answers, talk about the text passage, or generate more words containing the root.

**3.** After students have discussed the Activate questions, invite whole-group conversation. You may wish to have students write down the shared ideas to revisit at a later time.

## Divide and Conquer: Base sed-, sid-, sess-

**4.** As you guide students through Divide and Conquer, use questions like these to generate discussion about each of the words:

- Where is the meaning of "sit" or "settle" in the word _____?

- Where might you see the word _____?

- Can you think of an example of _____?

- Does _____ have more than one meaning? If so, how are those meanings the same? How are they different?

- How is the word _____ different from the word _____?

- What words do you know of that have sed-, sid-, or sess- in them? What do these words have to do with "sit" or "settle"?

- Does the word have a suffix? (Students respond.) If yes, what does the suffix do? Can you think of other words that have this suffix?

## Making Connections: Magic Square

**5.** Students can work independently or with partners to complete the Magic Square. If this type of activity is new for them, make sure they understand the directions, including how they can check their answers mathematically (all rows and columns will add up to the same number).

---

### Words with sed-, sid-, sess-

| | |
|---|---|
| assess | possession |
| assessed | preside |
| assessing | reside |
| assessment | sedate |
| assessor | sedentary |
| assiduous | sediment |
| possess | session |
| possessed | subside |
| possessing | supersede |

To print a full list of words for students, see page 150.

---

Name: _____    Date: _____

## About the Root:
# Base sed-, sid-, sess-

## Activate

**Directions:** Some *sed-*, *sid-*, *sess-* words describe literal (actual) "sitting" or "settling," but many describe "sitting" in a figurative (not actual) sense. Talk with a partner to decide whether each underlined word in each phrase below represents a literal or a figurative sitting/settling.

1. <u>sediment</u> at the bottom of a river

2. place of <u>residence</u>

3. <u>sedentary</u> job

4. heavy rains <u>subside</u>

## Respond

**Directions:** Read the passage on page 35. Then answer the question below.

5. Do you think it is right to trick tax assessors? Why or why not?

_____

_____

_____

_____

_____

_____

## About the Root:
# Base sed-, sid-, sess- (cont.)

# Tax Assessors

People who own property usually pay real estate taxes to their local communities. Real estate refers to the land a person owns and any buildings on it. The property owner is required to pay taxes on it, whether or not the owner *resides* there. An assessor calculates the amount to be paid.

The word *assessor* has an interesting history that deals with "sitting." In 14th-century France, the assessor was an assistant judge. People would appear in court and argue their cases. While the judge listened, an assistant would "sit" by his side to compute the taxes and fees owed by the individual. The total charges computed by the assessor amounted to that individual's tax *assessment*.

Today, tax assessors are the specialists who calculate the worth of property. This assessment is then used to determine the amount of property tax the owner must pay. Property taxes are usually charged annually. And every few years, properties are *reassessed* to reflect changes in the value of real estate in the community.

Some property owners use tricks to try to reduce their taxes. For example, in 17th-century England, windows were taxed. Lots of homeowners simply boarded up their windows to avoid the tax. Likewise, some Midwestern farmers leave the outsides of their homes and farm buildings looking shabby. They hope that when the assessor drives by, he or she will think the property is worth far less than it actually is.

Name: _____  Date: _____

## Divide and Conquer:
## Base *sed-, sid-, sess-*

**Directions:** Complete the chart below. If a word does not have a prefix or a suffix, the chart is marked with X. Be sure to use *sit* or *settle* in your definitions. Then, write sentences on a separate sheet of paper, using two of the words from the chart. **Hint:** Three words have suffixes. One suffix makes the word an adjective (a describing word). In the other two cases, the suffix makes the word a noun (a person, place, thing, or idea).

| Word | Prefix Means | Base Means | Suffix Means | Definition |
|------|--------------|------------|--------------|------------|
| 1. residence | *re-* = back, again | | | |
| 2. president | *pre-* = before, in front of | | X | |
| 3. subside | *sub-* = below, under | | X | |
| 4. sedentary | X | | | |
| 5. session | X | | | |

Name: _____  Date: _____

## Making Connections:
# Magic Square

· · · · · · · · · · · · · · · · · · · · · · · · · · · · · · · · · · · · · · · · · · · · · · · · · ·

**Directions:** Match each word on the left to the sentence it completes on the right. Then put the numbers into the chart where they belong. Check your answers. If you are correct, all rows and columns will add up to the same "magic" number.

| | |
|---|---|
| _____ **A.** session | **1.** Franklin Delano Roosevelt was _6_ for 12 years, longer than any other person. |
| _____ **B.** sediment | **2.** Queen Elizabeth and her family _E_ in several palaces throughout Great Britain. |
| _____ **C.** obsessed | **3.** John Wilkes Booth was _____ with President Abraham Lincoln. |
| _____ **D.** multisession | **4.** The vice president _H_ over the Senate. |
| ✓ **E.** reside | **5.** The Speaker of the House of Representatives calls the Congress into _____. |
| _____ **F.** presides | **6.** Officials were unable to assess damage until the flood waters _____. |
| ✓ **G.** president | **7.** The National Guard helped remove the _____ left behind by the hurricane. |
| ✓ **H.** subsided | **8.** A tax _____ establishes the value of people's property. |
| _____ **I.** assessor | **9.** The candidate's trip to our city was a _____ event. She made five speeches! |

| | | |
|---|---|---|
| **A:** | **B:** | **C:** |
| **D:** | **E:** | **F:** |
| **G:** | **H:** | **I:** |

**Magic Number:**

_____

# Base duc-, duct-

## duc-, duct- = "lead"

## Standards

Uses a variety of context clues to decode unknown words

Determines the meaning of general academic and domain-specific words and phrases in a text relevant to a grade 5 topic or subject area

Reviews the key ideas expressed and draws conclusions in light of information and knowledge gained from the discussions

## Materials

- *About the Root: Base* duc-, duct- (pages 40–41)

- *Divide and Conquer: Base* duc-, duct- (page 42)

- *Making Connections: Authors and Illustrators* (page 43)

## Teaching Tips

- The Latin base *duc-, duct-* means "lead." Students may already know words built on this base. An orchestra *conductor*, for example, "leads" musicians "together" as they perform. Copper wires *conduct* electricity by "leading" the current along. The *ducts* in a heating system "lead" air from the furnace to the rooms. Prominent athletes may be *inducted* ("led into") into a Hall of Fame, and a child may be *abducted* ("led away") from the playground.

- *Duc-, duct-* appears in many social studies words. In European history, students learn about *dukes* and *duchesses* who are the political "leaders" of their regions (including Mussolini, Il Duce). The ancient Romans built elaborate *aqueducts* to "lead" "water" from the countryside into cities.

- Another interesting *duc-, duct-* word is *produce* (fruits and vegetables). The ancient Romans believed that Mother Earth "led" crops "forth" from the ground as she *produced* them and brought them into being (Latin prefix *pro-* = "forth," "forward," "ahead"). Today, we say that industries *produce* goods and manufacture *products*.

## Guided Practice

### About the Root: Base duc-, duct-

**1.** Write *air duct* on the board. Ask students to talk to partners to figure out the meaning of *duct-,* based on this example. Invite sharing. Explain that *duc-, duct-* means "lead."

**2.** Write the sentences *The child was ab<u>duct</u>ed* and *The researcher was in<u>duct</u>ed into the National Historical Society* on the board. Ask partners to use this information to figure out where the "lead" is in these words. After a couple of minutes, invite sharing. Stress the use of "lead" in students' responses.

# Base *duc-, duct-* (cont.)

**3.** Tell students that words with *duc-, duct-* often begin with a prefix. Write the prefixes *con-* = "with," "together" and *re-* = "back," "again" on the board. Ask students to brainstorm *duc-, duct-* words with each prefix (e.g., *conduct, conducive, reduce*). Ask them to explain how each word means "lead."

**4.** Ask students to complete the About the Root pages. They can work individually or with partners. After they have finished, invite whole-group conversation. Students can share answers, talk about the text passage, or generate more words containing the root.

**5.** After students have discussed the Activate activity, invite whole-group conversation. You may wish to have students write down the shared ideas to revisit at a later time.

## Divide and Conquer: Base *duc-, duct-*

**6.** As you guide students through Divide and Conquer, use questions like these to generate discussion about each of the words:

- Where is the meaning of "lead" in the word _____?

- Where might you see the word _____?

- Can you think of an example of _____?

- Does _____ have more than one meaning? If so, how are those meanings the same? How are they different?

- How is the word _____ different from the word _____?

- What other words do you know that contain this root? Do these words contain the essential meaning of the root?

- Does the word have a suffix? (Students respond.) If yes, what does the suffix do? Can you think of other words that have this suffix?

## Making Connections: Authors and Illustrators

**7.** Ask teams who drew/wrote about the same situation to show/read these aloud. The rest of the class can compare these two (or more) versions.

### Words with *duc-, duct-*

| | |
|---|---|
| abduct | educate |
| abduction | education |
| abductor | educator |
| aqueduct | induce |
| conducive | induct |
| conduct | induction |
| conduction | introduce |
| conductor | introduction |
| deduce | misconduct |
| deduct | product |
| deduction | reduction |
| duchess | seduce |
| duke | viaduct |

To print a full list of words for students, see page 150.

Name: _____   Date: _____

## About the Root:
# Base duc-, duct-

### Activate

**Directions:** Work with a partner to restate the sentences below by replacing each *duc-, duct-* word with its definition. Use "lead" in your definitions.

1. The new law about engine efficiency should help us *reduce* gas consumption.

2. The mayor *conducts* all meetings of the city council.

### Respond

**Directions:** Read the passage on page 41. Then answer the question below.

3. Why do you think ancient Romans built their aqueducts above ground?

_____

_____

_____

_____

_____

_____

_____

## About the Root:
# Base *duc-, duct-* (cont.)

# Aqueducts

An *aqueduct* is a water bridge. It's a channel, either narrow or wide, that conveys water from one place to another. Usually, aqueducts are built above ground, unlike ditches or canals, which are carved into the ground.

Aqueducts were introduced in ancient times. Many ancient civilizations developed them. However, they are usually associated with ancient Rome. Ancient Romans built aqueducts all over their empire. These aqueducts supplied water to cities far from the source so that people could more conveniently bathe and have drinking water. Historians believe that the ancient Romans' engineering feats were remarkable. What they did to produce aqueducts was not equaled for more than a thousand years.

Modern aqueducts are found all over the world. Like their ancient counterparts, they still *conduct,* or carry, water from one place to another where it is needed. For example, a 120-mile aqueduct starts in the Catskill Mountains. It ends in New York City, where it supplies water for many in that large urban area.

Aqueduct on the Oakland Canal.

Name: _____     Date: _____

## Divide and Conquer:
## Base *duc-*, *duct-*

**Directions:** Complete the chart below. If a word does not have a suffix, the chart is marked with X. Be sure to use *lead* in your definitions. Then, write sentences on a separate sheet of paper, using two of the words from the chart. **Hint:** Two suffixes mean "one who." Another suffix makes its word an adjective (a describing word). The fourth suffix makes its word a verb (an action word).

| Word | Prefix Means | Base Means | Suffix Means | Definition |
|------|--------------|------------|--------------|------------|
| 1. reduce | *re-* = back, again | | X | |
| 2. educate | *e-* = out of | | | |
| 3. introduce | *intro-* = inside, within | | X | |
| 4. conductor | *con-* = with, together | | | |
| 5. inductee | *in-* = in, on, into | | | |
| 6. productive | *pro-* = forth, forward, ahead | | | |

Name: _____  Date: _____

## Making Connections:
# Authors and Illustrators
· · · · · · · · · · · · · · · · · · · · · · · · · · · · · · · · · · · · · · · · · · · · · · · · · ·

**Directions:** You and a partner will be a team. Select one sentence and write a paragraph about it. Use as many *duc-*, *duct-* words as you can. Some suggestions are in parentheses.

Trade stories with another team. Read their story and draw a picture about some part of the story. Share your illustration and explain what you drew and why you chose that part. Listen as the other team shares what they drew and why.

> The *duke* and *duchess* visit with the queen. (introduce, introduction, archduke)

> Tourists view an ancient *aqueduct*. (conduct, introduce, introduction)

> The farm's *produce* is destroyed by grasshoppers. (production, reduce, reduction)

> The FBI foils an *abduction*. (abduct, abductor, misconduct)

> The member of Congress was censured for *misconduct*. (conduct, reduce, educate)

_____

_____

_____

_____

_____

_____

_____

# Suffixes -cracy and -crat

## -cracy = "rule by"

## -crat = "ruler"

## Standards

Uses phonetic and structural analysis techniques, syntactic structure, and semantic context to decode unknown words

Uses combined knowledge of all letter-sound correspondences, syllabication patterns, and morphology to read accurately unfamiliar multisyllabic words in context and out of context

Reviews the key ideas expressed and draws conclusions in light of information and knowledge gained from the discussions

## Materials

- *About the Root: Suffixes* -cracy *and* -crat (pages 46–47)

- *Divide and Conquer: Suffixes* -cracy *and* -crat (page 48)

- *Making Connections: Word Sort* (page 49)

## Teaching Tips

- The Greek suffix *-cracy* means "rule by" and the Greek suffix *-crat* means "ruler" or "one who believes in rule by." These suffixes appear in many words that describe systems of government and types of rulers.

- A *democracy*, for example, is a government founded on the principle of "rule by" (*-cracy*) the "people" (*dem[o]*). Similarly, a *plutocracy* is "rule by the wealthy" (*plut[o]-* = wealth), a *theocracy* is "rule by (the laws of) God and religion" (*the[o]-* = god) and *aristocracy* is "rule by the best (who identify themselves as owners of land and inherited wealth)" (*arist[o]* = best).

- Most words ending in *-cracy*, describing types of government, have corresponding nouns ending in *-crat*, indicating "one who believes in such rule" (e.g., *democrat, plutocrat, theocrat, aristocrat*). Words ending in the suffix *-crat* may be converted into adjectives with the addition of the suffix *-ic* (e.g., *democratic, aristocratic, autocratic*).

## Guided Practice

### About the Root: Suffixes -cracy and -crat

1. Review the concept of *suffix* (unit attached to the end of a word that affects its meaning). Write *cracy-* and *crat-* (and their definitions—"rule by" and "ruler/one who believes in rule by") on the board. Ask students to talk with a neighbor and come up with synonyms for the word *rule* (e.g., *control, boss, run, govern*). Ask students to share aloud.

# Suffixes -cracy and -crat (cont.)

**2.** Write the words *autocracy* and *autocrat* on the board. Ask students what familiar root is in each word (*auto-* = self). Ask them to talk with a neighbor and see if they can figure out what the two words mean (*autocracy* = "rule by," "self"; *autocrat* = "self," "ruler"). Invite sharing. Ask students to talk with partners again to answer the following questions: *Is the United States an* autocracy? *Why or why not?* After a minute or two, invite sharing.

**3.** Ask students to complete the About the Root pages. They can work individually or with partners. After they have finished, invite whole-group conversation. Students can share answers, talk about the text passage, or generate more words containing the root.

**4.** After students have discussed the Activate questions, invite whole-group conversation. You may wish to have students write down the shared ideas to revisit at a later time.

## Divide and Conquer: Suffixes -cracy and -crat

**5.** As you guide students through Divide and Conquer, use questions like these to generate discussion about each of the words:

- Where is the meaning of "rule by" or "ruler/one who believes in rule by" in the word _____?

- Where might you see the word _____?

- Can you think of an example of _____?

- How is the word _____ different from the word _____?

- What other words do you know that contain this root? Do these words contain the meaning of the root?

## Making Connections: Word Sort

**6.** Students can work independently or with partners. To conclude this activity, invite sharing and discussion.

---

### Words with -cracy, -crat

| | |
|---|---|
| androcracy | gerontocracy |
| aristocracy | gynecocracy |
| aristocrat | gynecracy |
| aristocratic | plutocracy |
| autocracy | plutocrat |
| autocrat | technocracy |
| autocratic | technocrat |
| bureaucracy | theocracy |
| bureaucrat | theocrat |
| democracy | |

To print a full list of words for students, see page 151.

---

Name: _____    Date: _____

## About the Root:
# Suffixes -cracy and -crat

> ### Activate
>
> **Directions:** *Plut(o)-* means "wealth" or "the wealthy." Think about the questions below. Discuss them with a partner.
>
> 1. What is a *plutocracy*?
>
> 2. What is a *plutocrat*?
>
> 3. Do you think the United States is a *plutocracy*? Why?

### Respond

**Directions:** Read the passage on page 47. Then answer the question below.

4. Do you think that wealth is an important or a good characteristic for a ruler? Why or why not?

_____

_____

_____

_____

_____

_____

## About the Root:
# Suffixes -cracy and -crat (cont.)

# Aristocracies

An *aristocracy* is a form of government. Literally, it means "rule by" "the best" people. These elite citizens are called *aristocrats*. Over the years, what people have defined as "the best" has changed.

Ancient Rome, for example, had an *aristocratic* ruling class called the *Patricians*. Only people who owned large estates of land and possessed inherited wealth from their fathers could belong to the aristocracy.

Beginning in the 16th century, aristocracy has come to mean "rule by the richest people." In 16th century France, wealthy noblemen ruled. They were privileged by birth and wealth. They believed that being the richest entitled them to rule others. No wonder they called themselves "the best"! This meaning of *aristocrat* is still used today to describe people who belong to grand, noble families.

Name: _____     Date: _____

### Divide and Conquer:
# Suffixes -cracy and -crat

**Directions:** Complete the chart below. Be sure to use *rule by, ruler,* or *one who believes in rule by* in your definitions.

| Word | Base Means | Suffix Means | Definition |
|---|---|---|---|
| 1. democracy | *dem(o)-* = the people | | |
| 2. aristocrat | *arist(o)-* = the best | | |
| 3. plutocrat | *plut(o)-* = wealth | | |
| 4. autocrat | *auto-* = self | | |
| 5. theocracy | *the(o)-* = God | | |

Discuss the questions below with a partner. Write your answers on a separate sheet of paper.

6. Why is the U.S. government considered a *democracy*?

7. Could a government be both an *autocracy* and an *aristocracy*? Explain.

Name: _____ Date: _____

## Making Connections:
# Word Sort

· · · · · · · · · · · · · · · · · · · · · · · · · · · · · · · · · · · · · · · · · · · · · · · · · · · · · · · · · · · · · · ·

**Directions:** Use the words in the Word Bank to complete the chart below.

**Word Bank**

| | | | |
|---|---|---|---|
| aristocracy | autocracy | bureaucracy | technocracy |
| aristocrat | autocrat | bureaucrat | technocrat |
| aristocratic | autocratic | bureaucratic | technocratic |

| Types of Organization or Government | Person | Adjective (Describing Word) |
|---|---|---|
| | | |
| | | |
| | | |
| | | |

**Directions:** Write a paragraph using at least three words from the Word Bank. See if you can put more than one word in a sentence.

_____

_____

_____

_____

_____

_____

_____

Name: _____   Date: _____

## Unit I Review:
# Crossword Puzzle

**Directions:** Use the words from the Word Bank and the clues below to complete the crossword puzzle on page 51.

### Word Bank

| | | | |
|---|---|---|---|
| abdication | addendum | aristocracy | production |
| abduction | address | assessor | residence |
| abolished | adjacent | bureaucrat | supersede |
| abstract | aqueducts | democrat | |

## Across

1. Most people think the work of a _____ is just unimportant, low-level busywork.

6. _____ is rare. Most often a new monarch replaces an old one because of death.

10. The new contract will _____ all previous contracts.

11. If you visit Europe, you can see _____ built during the Roman Empire.

## Down

2. Although many notions about forms of government are _____, some are concrete.

3. In some countries _____ and monarchy are both forms of government.

4. The Bill of Rights is an _____ to the Constitution.

5. _____ is a crime everywhere.

6. As a result of the Civil War, slavery was _____.

7. To register to vote, you must show proof of your _____.

8. Most people do not like the work of the tax _____.

9. A _____ can be either someone who believes in democracy or a member of a political party.

Name: _____ Date: _____

Unit I Review:
# Crossword Puzzle (cont.)

**Directions:** Use the words from the Word Bank and the clues on page 50 to complete the crossword puzzle below.

# Base center-, centr(i)-

## center-, centr(i)- = "center"

## Standards

Uses a variety of context clues to decode unknown words

Uses common, grade-appropriate Greek and Latin affixes and roots as clues to the meaning of a word

Reviews the key ideas expressed and draws conclusions in light of information and knowledge gained from the discussions

## Materials

- *About the Root: Base* center-, centr(i)- (pages 54–55)

- *Divide and Conquer: Base* center-, centr(i)- (page 56)

- *Making Connections: Magic Square* (page 57)

## Teaching Tips

- The Greek base *center-, centr(i)-* means "center." This base combines with many Greek and Latin prefixes and bases to generate words students may already know, although they may not associate these words with "center." For example, when we *concentrate*, we "center" our thoughts "together" (*con-* = "together") on one subject.

- This base appears in many science words:

  - In physics, objects rotating around a fixed center point exhibit both *centrifugal* force, which "flees the center," and *centripetal* force, which "seeks the center" (*fug-* = "flee"; *pet-* = "seek").

  - In astronomy, planet Earth follows a *heliocentric* orbit, "centered" around the sun. The moon follows a *geocentric* orbit, "centered" around the Earth (*heli[o]-* = "sun"; *ge[o]-* = "earth").

  - In earth science, we learn that earthquakes originate from a *hypocenter* below the earth's surface (*hypo-* = "under," "below"). The location exactly above this point on the Earth's surface is called the *epicenter* (*epi-* = "upon").

## Guided Practice

### About the Root: Base center-, centr(i)-

1. Write *center-, centr(i)-* on the board. Ask students to guess the meaning of this base. (They should quickly answer, "center.") Ask partners to talk about where the "center" is in the phrases *concentric circles* and *a person with centrist positions about an issue.*

# Base center-, centr(i)- (cont.)

**2.** As students share ideas about the "center" in the phrases, you may wish to point out that "center" can be either literal (e.g., *concentric circles*) or figurative (e.g., *centrist*).

**3.** Ask students to complete the About the Root pages. They can work individually or with partners. After they have finished, invite whole-group conversation. Students can share answers, talk about the text passage, or generate more words containing the root.

**4.** After students have discussed the Activate activity, invite whole-group conversation. You may wish to have students write down the shared ideas to revisit at a later time.

## Divide and Conquer: Base center-, centr(i)-

**5.** As you guide students through Divide and Conquer, use questions like these to generate discussion about each of the words:

- Where is the meaning of "center" in the word _____?

- Where might you see the word _____?

- Can you think of an example of _____?

- How is the word _____ different from the word _____?

- What other words do you know that contain this root? Do these words contain the meaning of the root?

- Does the word have a suffix? (Students respond.) If yes, what does the suffix do? Can you think of other words that have this suffix?

## Making Connections: Magic Square

**6.** Students can work independently or with partners to complete the Magic Square. If this type of activity is new for them, make sure they understand the directions, including how they can check their answers mathematically (all rows and columns will add up to the same number).

---

### Words with center-, centr(i)-

| | |
|---|---|
| amniocentesis | concentration |
| anthropocentric | concentric |
| anthropocentrism | eccentric |
| central | eccentricity |
| centric | egocentric |
| centrist | egocentricity |
| centrifugal | epicenter |
| centrifugation | geocentric |
| centrifuge | heliocentric |
| centripetal | hypocenter |
| concentrate | |

To print a full list of words for students, see page 151.

---

Name: _____ Date: _____

About the Root:
# Base center-, centr(i)-

## Activate

**Directions:** Think about how the meaning of *center* in each statement below is literal (actually means "center") or figurative (the idea of "center"). Explain your thinking with a partner.

1. <u>center</u> court in basketball

2. an <u>egocentric</u> person

3. the <u>epicenter</u> of an earthquake

## Respond

**Directions:** Read the passage on page 55. Then answer the question below.

4. Why would a pilot's or astronaut's training need to include time in a centrifuge?

_____

_____

_____

_____

_____

_____

_____

_____

About the Root:
# Base center-, centr(i)- (cont.)

## Centrifuges

A *centrifuge* is a piece of equipment that puts a substance into rotation around a fixed axis. As the centrifuge spins, *centrifugal* force (Latin base *fug-* = "flee," "fleeing the center") causes the substance in the centrifuge to separate. Lighter parts of the substance move outward and toward the top as heavier parts move inward and toward the bottom. The heavier parts are drawn inward by *centripetal* force (Latin base *pet-* = "seek," "center-seeking"). Today's centrifuges are powered by electric motors. Once, the apparatus was turned by hand.

Centrifuges were first used to separate cream from milk. Today they are used in biology, chemistry, and aeronautics. In biology, centrifuges are used to separate blood so that the proportion of red blood cells can be determined. These centrifuges are called *hematocrits* (*hemat[o]-* = "blood" + *crit-* = "separate"). In chemistry, centrifuges are used to separate isotopes. They are even used in uranium enrichment, a step in the creation of nuclear power. Centrifuges are also used in aeronautics. Pilots and astronauts undergo training in large centrifuges. This experience simulates the effects of gravity.

Name: _____     Date: _____

## Divide and Conquer:
## Base center-, centr(i)-

**Directions:** Complete the chart below. If a word does not have a suffix, the chart is marked with X. Be sure to use *center* in your definitions. Then, write sentences on a separate sheet of paper, using two of the words from the chart. **Hint:** Three words in this list end with the suffix *-ic*, which makes the words adjectives (describing words).

| Word | Prefix Means | Base Means | Suffix Means | Definition |
|------|--------------|------------|--------------|------------|
| 1. geocentric | *ge(o)-* = earth | | | |
| 2. heliocentric | *heli(o)-* = sun | | | |
| 3. hypocenter | *hypo-* = under, below | | X | |
| 4. concentric | *con-* = with, together | | | |
| 5. epicenter | *epi-* = upon, on, above | | X | |

Name: _____ Date: _____

## Making Connections:
# Magic Square

· · · · · · · · · · · · · · · · · · · · · · · · · · · · · · · · · · · · · · · · · · · · · · · ·

**Directions:** Match each word on the left to the sentence it completes on the right. Then put the numbers into the chart where they belong. Check your answers. If you are correct, all rows and columns will add up to the same "magic" number. (**Hint:** You will not use one of the numbered words.)

| | |
|---|---|
| _____ **A.** epicenter | 1. A _____ direction is one that moves toward the center. |
| _____ **B.** egocentric | 2. I accused my brother of being _____ because he always only thinks of himself. |
| _____ **C.** eccentric | 3. _____ force moves objects outward from the center of a spinning device. |
| _____ **D.** concentric | 4. _____ circles share the same center point. |
| _____ **E.** concentrated | 5. Is it possible to have _____ positions about global warming? |
| _____ **F.** centrifuges | 6. This orange juice is _____. We have to add water before drinking. |
| _____ **G.** centrist | 7. You could call my aunt _____. We just think her behavior is quirky. |
| _____ **H.** anthropocentric | 8. Pilots and astronauts often train in _____ to simulate the force of gravity in space. |
| _____ **I.** centrifugal | 9. The _____ of the earthquake was between Los Angeles and San Francisco. |
| _____ **J.** centripetal | 10. Someone with _____ beliefs thinks that human beings are the central element of the universe. |

| | | |
|---|---|---|
| A: | B: | C: |
| D: | E: | F: |
| G: | H: | I: |

**Magic Number:**

_____

# Base *audi-, audit-*

## *audi-* and *audit-* = "hear," "listen"

## Standards

Uses phonetic and structural analysis techniques, syntactic structure, and semantic context to decode unknown words

Determines the meaning of general academic and domain-specific words and phrases in a text relevant to a grade 5 topic or subject area

Reviews the key ideas expressed and draws conclusions in light of information and knowledge gained from the discussions

## Materials

- *About the Root: Base* audi-, audit- (pages 60–61)

- *Divide and Conquer: Base* audi-, audit- (page 62)

- *Making Connections: Scramble* (page 63)

## Teaching Tips

- The Latin base *audi-, audit-* means "hear," "listen." Students know words from this base, although they may not associate these words with "hearing" or "listening." For example, an *auditorium* is a large room where the *audience* can "hear" speakers and performers.

- This base appears in many science words:

  - *Audible* sounds are within normal "hearing" range.

  - *Inaudible* sounds cannot be "heard" (*in-* = "not").

  - An *audiometer* measures a person's "hearing" ability.

  - An *audiologist* specializes in diagnosing and treating "hearing" problems.

  - *Auditory* nerves enable us to "hear."

## Guided Practice

### About the Root: Base *audi-, audit-*

1. On the board, write the sentence *Dog whistles are* <u>audible</u> *if you are a dog but are* <u>inaudible</u> *if you are a human.* Ask partners to discuss the underlined parts of the words. Ask, "What does *audi-* mean?"

2. After a minute or two, invite sharing. Point out that *audi-* means "hear" or "listen."

3. Ask students to complete the About the Root pages. They can work individually or with partners. After they have finished, invite whole-group conversation. Students can share answers, talk about the text passage, or generate more words containing the root.

# Base audi-, audit- (cont.)

**4.** After students have discussed the Activate activity, invite whole-group conversation. You may wish to have students write down the shared ideas to revisit at a later time.

## Divide and Conquer: Base audi-, audit-

**5.** As you guide students through Divide and Conquer, use questions like these to generate discussion about each of the words:

- Where is the meaning of "hear," "listen" in the word _____?

- Where might you see the word _____?

- Can you think of an example of _____?

- How is the word _____ different from the word _____?

- What other words do you know that contain this root? Do these words contain the meaning of the root?

- Does the word have a suffix? (Students respond.) If yes, what does the suffix do? Can you think of other words that have this suffix?

## Making Connections: Scramble

**6.** Students can work independently or with partners. To conclude this activity, invite sharing.

---

**Words with audi-, audit-**

| | |
|---|---|
| audible | audiovisual |
| audience | audit |
| audio-lingual | audition |
| audiologist | auditor |
| audiology | auditorium |
| audiometer | auditory |
| audiotape | inaudible |

To print a full list of words for students, see page 152.

---

Name: _____  Date: _____

### About the Root:
# Base *audi-, audit-*

## Activate

**Directions:** Think about how the words below include the idea of hearing or listening. Explain your ideas to a partner.

1. audiotape

2. audience

3. audition

## Respond

**Directions:** Read the passage on page 61. Then answer the question below.

4. Loud and continual noise can damage hearing. What might an audiologist recommend in a noisy workplace?

_____

_____

_____

_____

_____

_____

## About the Root:
# Base audi-, audit- (cont.)

# Audiologists

You know that *audi-, audit-* means "hear" or "listen." From this, can you figure out what *audiology* is? It is the science of studying hearing. Scientists who are experts in audiology are called *audiologists*.

Audiologists are trained to diagnose, treat, and monitor *auditory* difficulties. They test to determine if their patients can hear sounds that most people can hear. They usually use *audiometers* to do this. An audiometer is a machine that measures hearing loss. Audiometers can show the range of a person's hearing difficulties. People may have difficulty with some or all of the following: high frequencies, middle frequencies, or low frequencies. If an audiologist detects problems, he or she will tell the patient about ways to solve the problem.

In addition to helping people with hearing difficulties, audiologists help to support hearing health. For example, some audiologists screen newborn babies' hearing. Others screen hearing in school-age children. Still others help to create rules for auditory safety in the workplace. All of these efforts aim to prevent hearing difficulties before they appear.

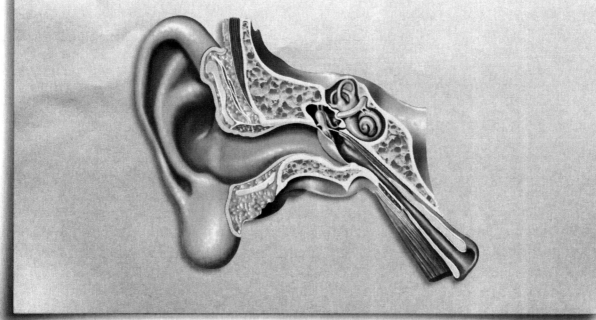

Name: _____ Date: _____

Divide and Conquer:
# Base *audi-, audit-*

**Directions:** Complete the chart below. Be sure to use *hear* or *listen* in your definitions.
**Hint:** One suffix means "able to be." One suffix makes its word a noun (a thing or idea). The third suffix means "of or relating to."

| Word | First Base Means | Second Base/ Suffix Means | Definition |
|---|---|---|---|
| 1. audible | | | |
| 2. audiophile | | *phil* = love | |
| 3. audiometer | | *meter* = measure | |
| 4. audition | | | |
| 5. auditory | | | |

Work with a partner to discuss the questions below. Write your answers on a separate sheet of paper.

6. How are *audible* and *inaudible* alike? How are they different?

7. Use two of the words from the chart in sentences.

Name: _____ Date: _____

## Making Connections:
# Scramble
..............................................................................

**Directions:** Unscramble the words to fill in the blanks.

1.  _____ equipment has both sound and visual components. (audioailsuv)

2.  The _____ for the scientist's speech was extremely interested in her topic. (audiceen)

3.  Would an _____ sound wake a sleeping baby? (audibeiln)

4.  Voice coaches help people learn to project their voices so they will be _____ in a large _____. (audibel, audiimortu)

5.  The _____ screened our hearing in school. The test didn't hurt and took only a couple of minutes. (audigiloost)

6.  An _____ measures a person's hearing. (audieemort)

7.  _____ learners learn best through hearing things. (audiorty)

8.  One method of learning a foreign language, called _____, relies mostly on listening and speaking. (audio-gaillnu)

**Directions:** Select two of the words from the Word Bank. Write sentences with blanks. Scramble the answers. Then give your sentences to a classmate. Ask him or her to unscramble the words to fill in the blanks.

| Word Bank | | | |
|---|---|---|---|
| audible | audience | audition | inaudible |

9.  _____

    _____

10. _____

    _____

# Base *pon-, pos-, posit-*

## *pon-, pos-, posit-* = "put," "place"

## Standards

Uses a variety of context clues to decode unknown words

Uses combined knowledge of all letter-sound correspondences, syllabication patterns, and morphology to read accurately unfamiliar multisyllabic words in context and out of context

Reviews the key ideas expressed and draws conclusions in light of information and knowledge gained from the discussions

## Materials

- *About the Root: Base pon-, pos-, posit-* (pages 66–67)

- *Divide and Conquer: Base pon-, pos-, posit-* (page 68)

- *Making Connections: Guess the Word* (page 69)

## Teaching Tips

- The Latin base *pon-, pos-, posit-* means "put" or "place." Students know words from this base, although they may not associate these words with "putting" or "placing." For example, when we *pose* for a picture, we "put" our head and shoulders in a fixed *position*. When we *post* a letter, we "put" it in a mailbox (hence, *Postal* Service). When we take a *position* on an issue, we "place" ourselves on one side.

- This base helps generate many science words:

  - A river *deposits* sediment at the bottom of the riverbed. These *deposits* have been "put" "down" by the slowing current. Over time, organic matter *decomposes* (*de-* = "down," "off").

  - We can suffer from frostbite if we *expose* (*ex-* = "out") our fingers to extremely low temperatures over a period of time.

  - Environmentally conscious people may *compost* their yard trimmings and leaves by "putting" all this organic matter "together" in a pile.

  - Researchers often *propose* scientific theories (*hypotheses*) for testing. A research *proposal* "puts forward" an idea for examination (*pro-* = "forth," "forward").

## Guided Practice

### About the Root: Base *pon-, pos-, posit-*

1. Write *pon-, pos-, posit-* on the board. Tell students that this Latin root means "put" or "place." Explain that it is used in many words they already know, but sometimes, figuring out how the words mean "put" or "place" is tricky. Ask them to figure out how the phrases com*post* pile (**Hint**: *com-* = "with" or "together") and de*posit* of sediment (**Hint**: *de-* = "away") include "put" or "place."

# Base pon-, pos-, posit- *(cont.)*

**2.** After a couple of minutes, ask students to share results. Reinforce the concept of "put" and "place" in their responses.

**3.** Ask students to complete the About the Root pages. They can work individually or with partners. After they have finished, invite whole-group conversation. Students can share answers, talk about the text passage, or generate more words containing the root.

**4.** After students have discussed the Activate activity, invite whole-group conversation. You may wish to have students write down the shared ideas to revisit at a later time.

## Divide and Conquer: Base pon-, pos-, posit-

**5.** As you guide students through Divide and Conquer, use questions like these to generate discussion about each of the words:

- Where is the meaning of "put," "place" in the word _____?

- Where might you see the word _____?

- Can you think of an example of _____?

- How is the word _____ different from the word _____?

- What other words do you know that contain this root? Do these words contain the meaning of the root?

- Does the word have a suffix? (Students respond.) If yes, what does the suffix do? Can you think of other words that have this suffix?

## Making Connections: Guess the Word

**6.** Students can work independently or with partners. To extend the activity, ask students to make new *pon-, pos-, posit-* words and to write riddles for them. Others can solve these riddles, either in small groups or as a whole group.

---

### Words with pon-, pos-, posit-

| | |
|---|---|
| component | oppose |
| compose | opposition |
| composite | pose |
| composition | posit |
| compost | position |
| depose | positive |
| deposit | postpone |
| dispose | posture |
| disposition | propose |
| expose | repose |
| exposition | repository |
| impose | superimpose |
| imposition | suppose |
| juxtapose | transpose |
| juxtaposition | |

To print a full list of words for students, see page 152.

---

Name: _____  Date: _____

About the Root:
# Base *pon-, pos-, posit-*

## Activate

**Directions:** As you now know, *pon-, pos-, posit-* means "put" or "place." Work with a partner to explain how each underlined word includes the idea of "put" or "place":

1. <u>Exposed</u> flesh easily freezes in very cold weather. (**Hint:** *ex-* means "out")

2. In science class last week, we made a chemical <u>composition</u>. (**Hint:** *com-* means "with" or "together")

## Respond

**Directions:** Read the passage on page 67. Then answer the question below.

3. Why would it be important for plant roots to hold dunes in position?

_____

_____

_____

_____

_____

_____

## About the Root:
# Base *pon-, pos-, posit-* (cont.)

# Sand Dunes

Imagine millions or even billions of grains of sand *deposited* in a particular spot. This would make a big hill of sand called a *sand dune*. Sand dunes are built by either wind or water flow. Dunes have different shapes and sizes because of differences in interactions with the flow of wind or water.

Sand dunes tend to be gradually sloped on the side the wind first hits. The other side of the dune tends to have fewer sand *deposits*, so its shape drops off quickly. Dunes caused by water run parallel to the shoreline. They may shift location and size with changes in wave motion and the rising and falling of the tides.

Sand dunes are *composed* of much more than sand. Plants and animals, both those we can see and tiny ones hidden in the sand, live in dunes. When a dune first forms near the ocean, conditions on it are harsh. Much of the sand and many of the crushed shells are covered with seawater, which makes it difficult for plants to survive. But rotten seaweed is also generally part of new dunes; this is like *compost*. It provides rich nutrients for plant growth. Eventually, many types of sea grass grow in dunes. This is both beautiful and important. The roots from the grasses help hold the dunes in *position*.

Name: _____ Date: _____

## Divide and Conquer:
# Base *pon-, pos-, posit-*

**Directions:** Complete the chart below. If a word does not have a prefix or suffix, the chart is marked with X. Be sure to use *place* or *put* in your definitions. Then, write sentences on a separate sheet of paper, using two of the words from the chart. **Hint:** Two suffixes make the words nouns (people, places, things, or ideas). The *-ite* in *composite* makes the word an adjective (a describing word).

| Word | Prefix Means | Base Means | Suffix Means | Definition |
|---|---|---|---|---|
| 1. compost | *com-* = with, together | | X | |
| 2. deposit | *de-* = down, off | | X | |
| 3. position | X | | | |
| 4. expose | *ex-* = out | | X | |
| 5. opponent | *op- (ob-)* = up against | | | |
| 6. composite | *com-* = with, together | | | |

Name: _____ Date: _____

## Making Connections:
# Guess the Word

· · · · · · · · · · · · · · · · · · · · · · · · · · · · · · · · · · · · · · · · · · · · · · · · · · ·

**Directions:** Use the words in the Word Bank to solve the riddles below.

> **Word Bank**
>
> compose          decompose          exposure
> composition      decomposition      oppose
> compost          deposit            positive
>                  dispose

1. I am a verb. I mean "to make up," "to put together," or "to create." I have two syllables and one prefix. _Compose_

2. I am a verb. I mean "to rot" or "decay." I have two prefixes. I have three syllables. I am the opposite of #1. _decompose_

3. I am a noun. I am the process described in #2. I have five syllables. _decomposition_

4. I am a verb. I could mean "to lay down" or "leave behind." Waves may do this to sediment they leave behind. I have three syllables. _deposit_

5. I am a noun. I am organic matter. I am used for fertilizer. I have two syllables. _Compost_

6. I am a verb. I mean "to get rid of something." Scientists do me with chemicals and other environmental threats. I have two syllables and a prefix. _dispose_

7. I am a verb. I mean "to be against" or "resist." I have two syllables. _oppose_

8. I am an adjective. In physics or chemistry I am one kind of charged atom or group of atoms. My opposite is negative. I have three syllables. _positive_

9. I am a noun. If you are out in the sun, too much of me is dangerous for your skin. I have one prefix and three syllables. _exposure_

10. I am a noun with four syllables. When you measure the amount of fat versus the amount of lean mass in your body, you are measuring this. _Composition_

#50865—Getting to the Roots of Content-Area Vo

# Bases *aqua-* and *hydr(o)-*

**aqua- and hydr(o)- = "water"**

## Standards

Uses phonetic and structural analysis techniques, syntactic structure, and semantic context to decode unknown words

Uses common, grade-appropriate Greek and Latin affixes and roots as clues to the meaning of a word

Reviews the key ideas expressed and draws conclusions in light of information and knowledge gained from the discussions

## Materials

- *About the Root: Bases* aqua- *and* hydr(o)- (pages 72–73)

- *Divide and Conquer: Bases* aqua- *and* hydr(o)- (page 74)

- *Making Connections: Drawing and Acting* (page 75)

## Teaching Tips

- The Latin base *aqua-* and the Greek base *hydr(o)-* both mean "water." Students already know words built on these bases (e.g., *aquarium* [-arium = container], *aquatic; fire hydrant*).

- Greek *hydr(o)-* is in many specialized words:

  - *Hydrogen:* an element essential for the production of water, as in "$H_2O$" (*gen-* = "produce," "give birth"). *Hydrogen* "produces water."

  - *Hydrate:* to supply a body with water.

  - *Dehydrate:* to deprive of water (*de-* = "down," "off").

  - *Rehydrate:* to replenish with water (*re-* = "back," "again").

  - *Hydroelectric:* refers to the production of electricity by the power of running water.

  - *Hydrophobia:* the disease of rabies, characterized by "fear of water" in the affected animal (*-phobia* = "fear of").

  - *Hydroplane:* As a noun, it is a plane that can land on water. As a verb, it means to skid on the surface of water (*plan-* = "wander").

  - *Hydrotherapy:* the use of water to treat diseases or rehabilitate patients (*therap-* = "cure," "heal").

  - *Hydrosphere:* the aqueous vapor of Earth's atmosphere that includes all bodies of water and aqueous vapors (*spher-* = "sphere," "globe").

**Note:** With two exceptions (*rehydrate; rehydration* and *dehydrate; dehydration*), the bases *hydr(o)-* and *aqua-* appear in words without prefixes.

## Guided Practice

### About the Root: Bases *aqua-* and *hydr(o-)*

1. Write *aqua-* and *hydr(o)-* on the board. Also write the sentences *We saw aquatic animals when our class visited the aquarium* and *The generator near the dam creates hydroelectric power.*

# Bases *aqua-* and *hydr(o)-* (cont.)

**2.** Ask partners to figure out what the roots *aqua-* and *hydr(o)-* mean. Invite sharing. Point out that these roots, one from Latin and one from Greek, mean the same thing: "water."

**3.** Draw students' attention to the *o* in *hydroelectric*. Explain that many Greek bases have a "connecting *o*" to make them easier to pronounce. When working with Greek-based vocabulary, students should be on the lookout for the "connecting *o*" to help them "divide and conquer" long words.

**4.** Ask students to complete the About the Root pages. They can work individually or with partners. After they have finished, invite whole-group conversation. Students can share answers, talk about the text passage, or generate more words containing the root.

**5.** After students have discussed the Activate questions, invite whole-group conversation. You may wish to have students write down the shared ideas to revisit at a later time.

## Divide and Conquer: Bases *aqua-* and *hydr(o-)*

**6.** As you guide students through Divide and Conquer, use questions like these to generate discussion about each of the words:

- Where is the meaning of "water" in the word _____?
- Where might you see the word _____?
- Can you think of an example of _____?
- How is the word _____ different from the word _____?
- What other words do you know that contain this root? Do these words contain the meaning of the root?
- Does the word have a suffix? If yes, what does the suffix do? Can you think of other words that have this suffix?

## Making Connections: Drawing and Acting

**7.** To conclude these activities, invite sharing that focuses on the processes students used to complete the tasks. Draw students' attention to the meaning of "water" in the selected words. Ask how their sketches/skits would be different if no "water" were implied.

### Words with *aqua-*, *hydr(o)-*

| | |
|---|---|
| anhydrous | hydrant |
| aqua | hydrate |
| aquaculture | hydraulic |
| aqualung | hydrochloric |
| aquamarine | hydroelectricity |
| aquarium | hydrogen |
| Aquarius | hydrogenize |
| aquatic | hydrolysis |
| aqueduct | hydrophilic |
| aqueous | hydrophobic |
| aqueous humor | hydroponics |
| aquifer | hydrosphere |
| carbohydrates | hydrous |
| dehydrate | rehydrate |

To print a full list of words for students, see page 153.

Name: _____ Date: _____

About the Root:

# Bases aqua- and hydr(o)-

## Activate

**Directions:** Think about the question below. Discuss it with a partner.

1. Why do you think we have two different roots from two different languages that mean the same thing?

## Respond

**Directions:** Read the passage on page 73. Then answer the question below.

2. Do you think the advantages of hydroponics outweigh its disadvantages? Explain your thinking.

_____

_____

_____

_____

_____

_____

_____

## About the Root:
# Bases aqua- and hydr(o)- (cont.)

# Hydroponics

Can you grow plants without soil? Perhaps you have rooted a new plant in water. An avocado seed will sprout roots if it is partially submerged in water. These are examples of *hydroculture*, which is *aquatic* agriculture (*agri-*, by the way, means "field").

*Hydroponics* is one type of hydroculture. It's a way to grow plants using nutrients dissolved in water. Roots of a plant grown *hydroponically* may simply float in water. Or they may be rooted in an inert medium like gravel or clay.

Scientists of the 18th century discovered that plants could absorb nutrients directly from water. Under the right conditions, then, soil is not needed to grow plants. Light is needed, of course, and nutrients need to be added to water. Occasionally, the water needs to be aerated (supplied with air).

Like many agricultural options, hydroponics has both advantages and disadvantages. Among the advantages are no need for pesticides, uniform yield, easy harvest, and reuse of water. The chief disadvantage is that if any difficulty arises, hydroponic plants die very quickly.

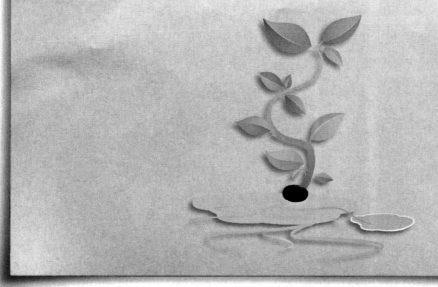

Name: _____    Date: _____

## Divide and Conquer:
# Bases aqua- and hydro-

**Directions:** Complete the chart below. If a word does not have a second base or suffix, the chart is marked with X. Be sure to use *water* in your definitions. Then, write sentences on a separate sheet of paper, using two of the words from the chart. **Hint:** One suffix means "full of." The other suffix makes the word an adjective (a describing word).

| Word | First Base Means | Second Base Means | Suffix Means | Definition |
|------|------------------|-------------------|--------------|------------|
| 1. aqueous | | X | | |
| 2. hydroplane | | *-plane* = wander | X | |
| 3. hydrophobia | | *-phobia* = fear of | X | |
| 4. aquatic | | X | | |
| 5. hydrogen | | *-gen* = produce, give birth | X | |

Name: _____    Date: _____

## Making Connections:
# Drawing and Acting

**Part 1:** Drawing

**Directions:** Select two items from the boxes below to draw. See if your partner can figure out what they are.

| aquatic animal | semiaquatic animal | hydroplane | fire hydrant |

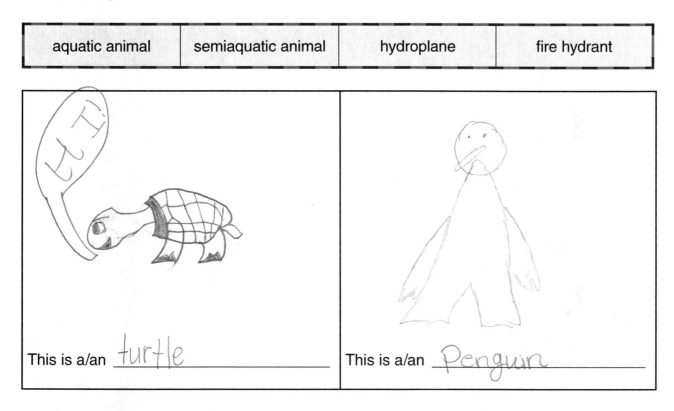

This is a/an ___turtle___          This is a/an ___Penguin___

**Part 2:** Word Skits

**Directions:** With one or more partners, choose a word from the list below. Write the word and its definition on an index card. Work together to create a skit to show the meaning of the word without talking. You may wish to create a tableau—turn yourselves into statues that display the meaning. Show your skit to others. See if they can guess your word

**Word Bank**

| aquarium | aqueduct | dehydrate |
| aquatic | carbohydrates | fire hydrant |

76

# Bases *dent-* and *odont-*

## dent- and odont- = "tooth," "teeth"

## Standards

Uses a variety of context clues to decode unknown words

Determines the meaning of general academic and domain-specific words and phrases in a text relevant to a grade 5 topic or subject area

Reviews the key ideas expressed and draws conclusions in light of information and knowledge gained from the discussions

## Materials

- *About the Root: Bases* dent- *and* odont- (pages 78–79)

- *Divide and Conquer: Bases* dent- *and* odont- (page 80)

- *Making Connections: Word Sort* (page 81)

## Teaching Tips

- The Latin base *dent-* and the Greek base *odont-* both mean "tooth" or "teeth." Latin base *dent-* appears in such words as *dentist, dental, dentistry,* and *dentures.* The Greek base *odont-* is easily recognized in such words as *orthodontics,* the specialty of straightening [teeth] (*orth[o]-* = "straight," "right").

- *Dent-* appears in specialized terminology. For example, *dentition* refers to the formation and so-called "cutting" of teeth. *Dentifrice* is the technical term for toothpaste or tooth powder which is "rubbed" on the teeth for cleaning (*fric-* = "rub"). *Dent-* even appears in commercial products associated with teeth (e.g., *Trident* chewing gum, *Fixadent*).

- In a few words, the Latin base *dent-* provides the figurative meaning of "teeth." These following words have interesting etymologies:

  A *trident* is a harpoon with three prongs that merely resemble teeth.

  When we *indent* a paragraph, we inset the first line, which looks as if someone bit "into" it with his or her teeth (Latin prefix *in-* = "in," "on," "into").

  In European history, an *indentured* servant would sign a contract for a loan from a property owner. The written agreement would be torn into two pieces, using the money-lender's teeth. If the borrower failed to repay the loan, he or she would become an "indentured servant" and perform manual labor until the debt was paid in full.

- The Greek base *odont-* appears in words dealing with technical or specialized aspects of dental sciences:

  *Orthodontics:* the medical specialty of straightening teeth, correcting bites, etc.

  *Periodontics:* the medical specialty and treatment of gums, (the membranes surrounding the teeth) (*peri-* = "around").

  *Exodontist:* a specialist in tooth extraction (*ex[o]-* = "out").

  *Pedodontist:* one who specializes in the teeth of children (*ped-* = "child").

  *Odontalgia:* technical term for tooth pain (*alg-* = "pain").

# Bases *dent-* and *odont-* (cont.)

## Guided Practice

### About the Root: Bases *dent-* and *odont-*

**1.** Write these sentences on the board: *I visit my <u>dent</u>ist twice each year, My brother needs braces, so he will work with an ortho<u>dont</u>ist,* and *My grandmother has <u>dent</u>ures now because her actual teeth no longer worked well.*

**2.** Have students work with partners to figure out what *dent-, odont-* might mean. Invite sharing. Explain that these bases mean "tooth" or "teeth."

**3.** Ask students to complete the About the Root pages. They can work individually or with partners. Invite whole-group conversation. Students can share answers, talk about the text passage, or generate more words containing the root.

**4.** After students have discussed the Activate activity, invite whole-group conversation. You may wish to have students write down the shared ideas to revisit at a later time.

> ### Words with *dent-, odont-*
>
> | | |
> |---|---|
> | dental | endodontist |
> | dentate | exodontist |
> | dentifrice | indent |
> | dentine | indentured |
> | dentist | orthodontist |
> | dentition | pedodontist |
> | dentoid | periodontist |
> | denture | trident |
>
> To print a full list of words for students, see page 153.

### Divide and Conquer: Bases *dent-* and *odont-*

**5.** As you guide students through Divide and Conquer, use questions like these to generate discussion about each of the words:

- Where is the meaning of "tooth/teeth" in the word _____?

- Where might you see the word _____?

- Can you think of an example of _____?

- How is the word _____ different from the word _____?

- What other words do you know that contain this root? Do these words contain the meaning of the root?

- Does the word have a suffix? If yes, what does the suffix do? Can you think of other words that have this suffix?

### Making Connections: Word Sort

**6.** To conclude this activity, discuss the second sort. Ask students to share reasons for their choices. You may want to write the *dent-, odont-* words on the board and circle the base within each word.

Name: _____    Date: _____

About the Root:
# Bases dent- and odont-

## Activate

**Directions:** Discuss with a partner how the words below are related to one another. Use all three in sentences on a separate sheet of paper.

1. dentist

2. dental charts

3. dentistry

## Respond

**Directions:** Read the passage on page 79. Then answer the question below.

4. Why do you think dentures need to be cleaned as often as real teeth do?

_____

_____

_____

_____

_____

_____

### About the Root:
# Bases dent- and odont- (cont.)

# Dentures

*Dentures* are false teeth. They replace missing or diseased teeth. Dentures can be partial or complete. A person might have top dentures, bottom dentures, or a full set. Dentures can be implanted permanently. Complete or full dentures are usually removable.

People can lose their teeth for several reasons. Poor oral health eventually leads to diseased teeth, which may then need to be extracted. Sometimes, people lose teeth in accidents. People can be born with malformed teeth. Malnutrition can also cause tooth decay.

Partial dentures can be removable or fixed. They are for people who are missing only some of their teeth. They are made to look like the patient's other teeth. Fixed dentures, which are attached permanently, are more expensive but also more durable.

Many years ago, animal teeth or wood were used for dentures. Today, dentures are made of artificial materials. For full dentures, the process begins with a *dental* impression. This impression is used to make a stone model, which is covered in wax so that the teeth can be set into it. The *dentist* frequently checks with the patient to make sure that the dentures are comfortable and useful for biting and chewing.

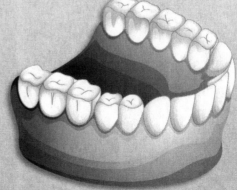

Dentures need to be cleaned just as natural teeth do. In fact, cleaning your teeth and visiting a dentist a couple of times each year is the best way to avoid needing dentures in the first place!

Name: _____     Date: _____

## Divide and Conquer:
# Bases *dent-* and *odont-*

**Directions:** Complete the chart below. If a word does not have a prefix or suffix, the chart is marked with X. Be sure to use *tooth* in your definitions. Then, write sentences on a separate sheet of paper, using two of the words from the chart. **Hint:** Two words have the same suffix, which means "one who." One word has a suffix that makes it a noun (an idea). The fourth suffix means "matters pertaining to."

| Word | Prefix Means | Base Means | Suffix Means | Definition |
|---|---|---|---|---|
| 1. exodontist | ex(o)- = out | | | |
| 2. trident | tri- = three | | X | |
| 3. periodontist | peri- = around | | | |
| 4. orthodontics | ortho- = straight | | | |
| 5. dentition | X | | | |

Name: _____   Date: _____

## Making Connections:
# Word Sort

· · · · · · · · · · · · · · · · · · · · · · · · · · · · · · · · · · · · · · · · · · · · · · · · · · · · ·

**Directions:** Write words from the Word Bank on the charts where they belong. Then fill the bottom chart with where the word part that means "tooth" is located.

| Word Bank | | | | |
|---|---|---|---|---|
| dental | dentist | indent | orthodontics | periodontics |
| dentifrice | dentures | mastodon | orthodontist | trident |

| Contains *dent-* | Contains *odont-* |
|---|---|
| dental | |
| dentifrice | |
| dentist | |
| dentures | |
| indent | |
| trident | |

| Is or Was Alive | Is Not Alive |
|---|---|
| | |
| | |
| | |
| | |
| | |
| | |

| Beginning of Word | Middle of Word | End of Word |
|---|---|---|
| | | |
| | | |
| | | |
| | | |

Name: _____     Date: _____

## Unit II Review:
# Crossword Puzzle

· · · · · · · · · · · · · · · · · · · · · · · · · · · · · · · · · · · · · · · · · · · · · · ·

**Directions:** Use the words in the Word Bank and the clues to complete the crossword puzzle on page 83.

### Word Bank

| | | | |
|---|---|---|---|
| aquarium | centrifuge | dentures | ~~hydrated~~ |
| audiologist | centrist | deposits | hydrogen |
| audiometer | compost | epicenter | ~~inaudible~~ |
| | ~~dental~~ | ~~exposed~~ | |

### Across

4. It's important to stay _____ while exercising, so drink lots of water!

5. _____ skin can burn in the summer and freeze in very cold weather.

6. Brushing and flossing are two important parts of _____ health.

10. Some sounds are _____ to the human ear, but they are still sounds.

11. A _____ can separate cream from milk.

12. _____ of sediment and other debris are left behind as glaciers melt.

### Down

1. The audiologist used an _____ to measure my hearing.

2. The _____ used an audiometer to measure my hearing.

3. _____ is rotted organic material that provides nutrients for gardens.

4. _____ is a chemical element with the symbol H.

6. _____ are false teeth.

7. What kinds of fish will you put in your new _____?

8. An earthquake emanates from its _____.

9. A person who holds moderate views on an issue is a _____.

Name: _____     Date: _____

## Unit II Review:
# Crossword Puzzle (cont.)

· · · · · · · · · · · · · · · · · · · · · · · · · · · · · · · · · · · · · · · · · · · · · · · · · · · · · · · · · · ·

**Directions:** Use the words in the Word Bank and the clues on page 82 to complete the crossword puzzle below.

# Prefix *dia-*

## dia- = "through," "across," "thorough"

## Standards

Uses phonetic and structural analysis techniques, syntactic structure, and semantic context to decode unknown words

Uses combined knowledge of all letter-sound correspondences, syllabication patterns, and morphology to read accurately unfamiliar multisyllabic words in context and out of context

Reviews the key ideas expressed and draws conclusions in light of information and knowledge gained from the discussions

## Materials

- *About the Root: Prefix* dia- (pages 86–87)
- *Divide and Conquer: Prefix* dia- (page 88)
- *Making Connections: Sketch to Stretch* (page 89)

## Teaching Tips

- The Greek prefix *dia-* means "through," "across," and "thorough." A *dialogue* is an extended conversation or discussion in which people "talk" "through" a topic (*log-* = "word," "speech"). The meanings "through" and "across" indicate direction, while the meaning "thorough" indicates intensity. They are, however, related. When something is "thoroughly" done, we say that it is done "through and through."

- In math, *dia-* refers to lines that cut all the way "through," "across" a geometric figure. Examples include:

  - *Diameter:* the line that cuts "through" the center of a circle from one side to the other (*meter-* = "measure"); other forms are *diametric* and *diametrically.*

  - *Diagonal:* a line that cuts all the way "through" a polygon, from one corner to the opposite one (*gon-* = "corner," "angle").

  - *Diagram:* a figure consisting of lines drawn "across" a page (*gram-* = "write," "draw").

- Students do not need to differentiate between whether *dia-* means "through," "across," or "thorough" in the individual words they work with. The goal is for them to associate all *dia-* words with the general sense of "through" (if providing direction) or "through and through" (if showing intensity).

## Guided Practice

### About the Root: Prefix *dia-*

1. Draw a circle on the board. Draw a diameter for the circle. Ask students, "What do we call this line bisecting the circle?"

# Prefix dia- *(cont.)*

**2.** Have students work with partners to write out a definition for *diameter*.

**3.** Invite students to share their written definitions, which will probably all contain the words *through* or *across*. Write *diameter* on the board. Underline *dia-* and tell students that this prefix means "through," "across."

**4.** Ask students to complete the About the Root pages. They can work individually or with partners. After they have finished, invite whole-group conversation. Students can share answers, talk about the text passage, or generate more words containing the root.

**5.** After students have discussed the Activate questions, invite whole-group conversation. You may wish to have students write down the shared ideas to revisit at a later time.

## Divide and Conquer: Prefix dia-

**6.** As you guide students through Divide and Conquer, use questions like these to generate discussion about each of the words:

- Where is the meaning of "through," "across," "thorough" in the word _____?

- Where might you see the word _____?

- Can you think of an example of _____?

- How is the word _____ different from the word _____?

- What other words do you know that contain this root? Do these words contain the meaning of the root?

- Does the word have a suffix? (Students respond.) If yes, what does the suffix do? Can you think of other words that have this suffix?

## Making Connections: Sketch to Stretch

**7.** Students can work independently or with partners. To conclude this activity, ask students to share their processes for deciding what to sketch.

---

### Words with dia-

| | |
|---|---|
| diabetes | diameter |
| diabetic | diametrically |
| diacritical | diaphanous |
| diagnose | diaphragm |
| diagonal | diarrhea |
| diagram | diatom |
| dialect | diatribe |
| dialogue | |

To print a full list of words for students, see page 154.

---

Name: _____     Date: _____

## About the Root:
# Prefix *dia-*

### Activate

**Directions:** Think about the questions below. Discuss them with a partner.

1. How does *diameter* represent "through," "across"?

2. How does *diagonal* represent "through," "across"?

### Respond

**Directions:** Read the passage on page 87. Then answer the question below.

3. Suppose that members of the high school marching band made a circle. They want you to figure out the circle's diameter. How would you do this?

_____

_____

_____

_____

_____

_____

_____

# About the Root:
## Prefix *dia-* (cont.)

# Diameters

In geometry, a *diameter* is any line segment that moves through the center point of a circle and ends on its edges. You could think of a diameter as the *diagonal* of a circle. With a measuring tape, you can estimate the diameter of circles from as small as a dime to as large as the top of a child's circular swimming pool.

But what if you wanted to figure out the diameter of something enormous? Something as big as Earth, for example? This is the challenge Eratosthenes (er-uh-TOS-thuh-neez) took on. He was an ancient Greek mathematician and scientist who lived around 250 B.C. He was a librarian and noticed that the sun came through the library windows at different angles in different places. This made him curious about how big Earth was.

Eratosthenes's plan involved two Egyptian cities. He measured the difference in the angles of the noonday sun in these two cities on the same day of the year. He knew the north-south distance between these cities. He assumed that Earth was round. Using the measurements and the assumption (and a lot of math), Eratosthenes estimated the diameter of Earth to be about 7,850 miles. Today, mathematicians and geographers believe the Earth is 7,900 miles in diameter. So the error in Eratosthenes's estimate was only a bit less than 2 percent. Amazing!

Name: _____   Date: _____

## Divide and Conquer:
## Prefix *dia-*

**Directions:** Complete the chart below. If a word does not have a suffix, the chart is marked with X. Be sure to use *through*, *across*, or *thorough* in your definitions. Then, write sentences on a separate sheet of paper, using two of the words from the chart. **Hint:** The suffix on one word makes it an adjective (a describing word).

| Word | Prefix Means | Base Means | Suffix Means | Definition |
|---|---|---|---|---|
| 1. diameter | | *-meter* = measure | X | |
| 2. diagnosis | | *-gnos* = know, read | X | |
| 3. diagram | | *-gram* = write, draw | X | |
| 4. diagonal | | *-gon* = angle, corner | | |
| 5. dialogue | | *-log-* = word, speech | X | |

Name: _____ Date: _____

## Making Connections:
# Sketch to Stretch

**Directions:** Here are five scenarios based on *dia-* words. Select three of them. Make a sketch of each scenario you choose in the boxes below. Then trade papers with a partner. See if they can match the sketches with the scenarios.

> ➤ A *dialect* is a form of speech used by a particular group. Before cars and airplanes, people who lived on either side of large mountains often spoke different dialects.
>
> ➤ Our community swimming pool is round. It takes me about two minutes to swim its *diameter*.
>
> ➤ Our one-story house is on a corner. The house *diagonal* to ours is also one story. The house across the street and its *diagonal* are both two stories.
>
> ➤ The architect's *diagram* for the new building was very detailed. It included a map of the lot and drawings of possible landscaping.
>
> ➤ Two characters in the play had an extended *dialogue* near the middle of the play. Their discussion back and forth went for more than five minutes!

# Prefixes peri-, circum- and circu-

## peri-, circum-, circu- = "around"

## Standards

Uses a variety of context clues to decode unknown words

Uses common, grade-appropriate Greek and Latin affixes and roots as clues to the meaning of a word

Reviews the key ideas expressed and draws conclusions in light of information and knowledge gained from the discussions

## Materials

- *About the Root: Prefixes* peri-, circum-, *and* circu- (pages 92–93)

- *Divide and Conquer: Prefixes* peri-, circum-, *and* circu- (page 94)

- *Making Connections: Scramble* (page 95)

## Teaching Tips

- The Greek prefix *peri-* and the Latin prefix *circum-, circu-* mean "around." The prefix *circum-, circu-* appears in words dealing with circles and round or curved figures or paths, such as:

  - *Circumference:* the measure of the external boundary of a circle.

  - *Circuit:* the path of an electrical current as it moves in a circle from pole to pole (*it-* = "go").

  - *Circulate:* to move in a circular path (as in the *circulation* of blood or the *circulatory* system).

  - *Circular:* shaped like a circle; round; also, a flyer or advertisement sent to customers who live "around" a store or location.

  - *Circumnavigate:* to sail around the globe (*navig-* = "sail").

  - *Circumambulate:* to walk around an area, as in a formal procession.

  - *Circumscribe:* to encircle by drawing a line around a figure (*scrib-* = "write, draw").

- The Greek prefix *peri-* appears in words describing polygons (consisting of straight lines and angles), in specialized medical terminology, and in words describing technical devices. Examples include:

  - *Perimeter:* the measurement around a polygon or other angular shape (*meter-* = "measure").

  - *Periscope:* a device on a submarine that looks around to see things above the ocean's surface (*scop-* = "look").

  - *Periodontics:* branch of dentistry dealing with the gums (membranes "around" the teeth; *odont-* = "tooth").

  - *Pericardium:* the membrane wrapped around the heart (*cardi-* = "heart").

# Prefixes *peri-*, *circum-* and *circu-* (cont.)

## Guided Practice

### About the Root: Prefix *peri-*, *circum-* and *circu-*

**1.** Write the prefixes *peri-*, *circum-*, and *circu-* on the board. Have partners answer the questions *How does the word circumference include the idea of "around"?* and *How does the word perimeter include the idea of "around"?* Invite discussion.

**2.** Ask students to complete the About the Root pages. They can work individually or with partners. After they have finished, invite whole-group conversation. Students can share answers, talk about the text passage, or generate more words containing the root.

**3.** After students have discussed the Activate activity, invite whole-group conversation. You may wish to have students write down the shared ideas to revisit at a later time.

### Divide and Conquer: Prefix *peri-*, *circum-* and *circu-*

**4.** As you guide students through Divide and Conquer, use questions like these to generate discussion about each of the words:

- Where is the meaning of "around" in the word _____?

- Where might you see the word _____?

- Can you think of an example of _____?

- How is the word _____ different from the word _____?

- What other words do you know that contain this root? Do these words contain the meaning of the root?

- Does the word have a suffix? (Students respond.) If yes, what does the suffix do? Can you think of other words that have this suffix?

### Making Connections: Scramble

**5.** To extend this activity, ask pairs of students to find a few more *peri-*, *circum-*, *circu-* words. They can write sentences with the target words scrambled. Have them trade papers with another pair of students to try to unscramble the words.

### Words with *peri-*, *circum-*, *circu-*

| | |
|---|---|
| circle | circumvent |
| circuit | semicircle |
| circular | pericardium |
| circulate | perigee |
| circumduct | perihelion |
| circumference | perimeter |
| circumnavigate | period |
| circumpolar | periodical |
| circumscribe | periodontics |
| circumspect | periphery |
| circumstance | periscope |

To print a full list of words for students, see page 154.

Name: _____   Date: _____

### About the Root:
# Prefixes *peri-*, *circum-* and *circu-*

## Activate

**Directions:** Think about the questions below. Discuss them and make the sketches with a partner.

1. Draw a semicircle on a separate sheet of paper. Show how the *semicircle* includes the idea of "around."

2. Sketch a running circuit for your school on a separate sheet of paper. How does a *circuit* include the idea of "around"?

## Respond

**Directions:** Read the passage on page 93. Then answer the question below.

3. Why do you think scientists and mathematicians have been so fascinated by the shape of circles?

   _____

   _____

   _____

   _____

   _____

   _____

**About the Root:**

# Prefixes *peri-, circum-* and *circu-* (cont.)

## Circles

*Circles* are important geometric shapes. They are two-dimensional. They are simple closed curves. They divide planes into two regions—inside and outside the circles. A circle is mathematically defined as all points in a plane that are the same distance from one point, the center of the circle.

People have been interested in circles since before recorded history. *Circular* shapes abound in nature—the sun, the moon, and even the shape of a plant stem if you cut through its middle. Even the wind often makes circles in the sand. Medieval scientists were fascinated with circles. In fact, some of these scientists considered circles to be intrinsically perfect.

Circles have been important to modern civilization, too. Where would we be without the wheel? And gears, important for engines of all kinds, are circular. In math, the circle helped interest scientists in the development of geometry and even advanced mathematics like calculus.

Many other shapes are circular or partially circular. Consider balls, globes, or bubbles, which are three-dimensional spheres but circular in shape. The numbers 8 and 9 have circular shapes, as do several letters of the alphabet. Circles are everywhere!

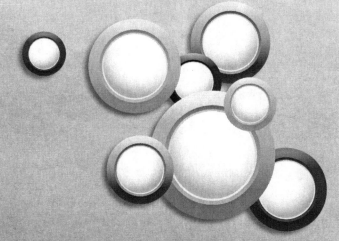

Name: _____     Date: _____

Divide and Conquer:

# Prefixes *peri-*, *circum-*, and *circu-*

**Directions:** Complete the chart below. If a word does not have a suffix, the chart is marked with X. Be sure to use *around* in your definitions. Then, write sentences on a separate sheet of paper, using two of the words from the chart. **Hint:** One suffix makes the word a noun (a thing or idea). One suffix makes the word an adjective (a describing word). The third suffix makes its word a verb (an action word).

| Word | Prefix Means | Base Means | Suffix Means | Definition |
|------|-------------|-----------|-------------|-----------|
| 1. perimeter | | -*meter* = measure | X | |
| 2. circumference | | -*fer* = bear, carry, take | | |
| 3. circuitous | | -*it* = go | | |
| 4. periscope | | -*scop* = look, watch | X | |
| 5. circumnavigate | | -*navig* = sail | | |

Name: _____     Date: _____

## Making Connections:
# Scramble

· · · · · · · · · · · · · · · · · · · · · · · · · · · · · · · · · · · · · · · · · · · · · · · · · · · · · · · · · · ·

**Directions:** Unscramble the *peri-*, *circum-*, *circu-* words to fill in the blanks.

1. Portuguese explorer Ferdinand Magellan _____ the globe when he sailed all the way around the world. (circumaaegintvd)

2. A circle has 360 degrees, but a _____ has 180 degrees. (eimscircel)

3. To determine the _____ of a geometric shape, add together the length of all its sides. (perieemrt)

4. A _____ allows people in a submarine to look around above the water. (periceops)

5. A _____ shape is round. (accilrru)

6. _____ vision allows you to see out of the corners of your eyes. (periaehlpr)

7. The _____ of a circle is the measurement around it. (circumceeefnr)

8. In science, we learned about the _____ system, which includes veins and arteries. (circualorty)

9. If you draw a circle around something, you _____ it. (cceeilnr)

10. Magazines are sometimes called _____. (periacdilos)

# Bases tempor- and chron(o)-

## tempor- and chron(o)- = "time"

## Standards

Uses phonetic and structural analysis techniques, syntactic structure, and semantic context to decode unknown words

Determines the meaning of general academic and domain-specific words and phrases in a text relevant to a grade 5 topic or subject area

Reviews the key ideas expressed and draws conclusions in light of information and knowledge gained from the discussions

## Materials

- *About the Root: Bases* tempor- *and* chron(o)- (pages 98–99)

- *Divide and Conquer: Bases* tempor- *and* chron(o)- (page 100)

- *Making Connections: Wordless Skits* (page 101)

## Teaching Tips

- The Latin base *tempor-* and the Greek base *chron(o)-* both mean "time." Students will know some *tempor-* words. *Temporary* measures, for example, are intended to last "for the time being." People who go "with the times" prefer *contemporary* fashions (*con-* = "with," "together"). Similarly, those who are born "with" us in the same "time" period are called our *contemporaries*. In music, we may tap our feet to the *tempo* and "keep time" with the song. When we speak *extemporaneously*, we do so without preparing in advance, speaking only "out of the time" allotted to us (*ex-* = "out").

- The Greek base *chron(o)-* appears in more specialized "time" words. In medicine, a *chronic* condition endures over an extended period of time. In studying history, we pay strict attention to the *chronology* of events as they occur over time (*-ology* = "study of") and in *chronological* order. People may *synchronize* their watches so that "together" they have the exact same time (*syn-* = "with," "together"); events that take place at the same time are called *synchronous*. A *chronometer* is a precise kind of timekeeper with a special mechanism to ensure accuracy in measurements of time and longitude at sea.

- To facilitate pronunciation, the final *o* of Greek bases may serve as a connecting vowel (e.g., the *o* in *chronological*). When working with Greek-based vocabulary, students should look for the "connecting o" to help them "divide and conquer" long words.

# Bases tempor- and chron(o)- (cont.)

## Guided Practice

### About the Root: Bases tempor- and chron(o)-

**1.** Write *tempor-* and *chron(o)-* on the board. Tell students that these roots have the same meaning. Write the phrases *tempor*ary password, *chron*ic headache, and *sy*n*chron*ized swimming (**Hint**: *syn-* means "with," "together") on the board. Tell students to chat with partners to figure out what the roots mean. Invite sharing. Explain that the bases mean "time."

**2.** Ask students to complete the About the Root pages. They can work individually or with partners. After they have finished, invite whole-group conversation. Students can share answers, talk about the text passage, or generate more words containing the root.

**3.** After students have discussed the Activate activity, invite whole-group conversation. You may wish to have students write down the shared ideas to revisit at a later time.

### Divide and Conquer: Bases tempor- and chron(o)-

**4.** As you guide students through Divide and Conquer, use questions like these to generate discussion about each of the words:

- Where is the meaning of "time" in the word _____?
- Where might you see the word _____?
- Can you think of an example of _____?
- How is the word _____ different from the word _____?
- What other words do you know that contain this root? Do these words contain the meaning of the root?
- Does the word have a suffix? If yes, what does the suffix do? Can you think of other words that have this suffix?

### Making Connections: Word Skits

**5.** Provide students time to plan before they perform their skits. At the conclusion of the skits, invite whole-group conversation about how they decided on their skits.

## Words with tempor-, chron(o)-

| | |
|---|---|
| anachronism | extemporaneous |
| anachronistic | extemporary |
| asynchronous | extemporize |
| chronic | spatiotemporal |
| chronicle | synchronize |
| chronograph | synchronous |
| chronological | tempo |
| chronology | temporal |
| chronometer | temporarily |
| chronometry | temporary |
| chronoscope | unsynchronized |
| contemporary | |

To print a full list of words for students, see page 155.

Name: _____        Date: _____

## About the Root:
# Bases tempor- and chron(o)-

## Activate

**Directions:** Define each phrase below with a partner. Be sure to use the word *time* in your definition.

1. <u>tempo</u>rary password

2. <u>chron</u>ic headache

3. syn<u>chron</u>ized swimming (**Hint:** *syn-* = "with," "together")

## Respond

**Directions:** Read the passage on page 99. Then answer the question below.

4. Why would playing computer games affect a person's spatiotemporal reasoning ability?

   _____

   _____

   _____

   _____

   _____

   _____

   _____

## About the Root:
# Bases *tempor-* and *chron(o)-* (cont.)

## Spatiotemporal Reasoning

Imagine you are holding a block with the letter *A* facing you. Now rotate the block in your mind, and try to keep track of where the face with the letter *A* is. If you did well with this task, you probably have good *spatiotemporal* reasoning ability. This is the ability to think about and visualize two- and three-dimensional figures in space (spati[o]) and time (temporal).

Studies have shown that younger people tend to have better spatiotemporal reasoning ability than older people. Males tend to be better at these types of tasks than females, too. However, scientists believe that practice may affect a person's spatiotemporal reasoning ability. In one study, males and females played computer games requiring spatiotemporal reasoning. After a few hours, their spatiotemporal reasoning was tested. No gender differences were found.

Website designers often consider users' spatiotemporal reasoning ability. It's important that sites be easy to navigate. Moreover, people should be able to find what they need on the site with little difficulty. End-user research helps designers develop sites that people with both weak and strong spatiotemporal reasoning ability can use successfully.

Name: _____   Date: _____

## Divide and Conquer:
# Bases tempor- and chron(o)-

**Directions:** Complete the chart below. If a word does not have a prefix or suffix, the chart is marked with X. Be sure to use *time* in your definitions. Then, write sentences on a separate sheet of paper, using two of the words from the chart. **Hint:** Three words have suffixes that make them adjectives (describing words). One word has a suffix that makes it a verb (an action word).

| Word | Prefix Means | Base Means | Suffix Means | Definition |
|------|-------------|-----------|-------------|-----------|
| 1. contemporary | con- = with, together | | | |
| 2. chronic | X | | | |
| 3. temporary | X | | | |
| 4. synchronize | syn- = with, together | | | |
| 5. chronicles | X | | X | |

Name: _____ Date: _____

## Making Connections:
# Wordless Skits

· · · · · · · · · · · · · · · · · · · · · · · · · · · · · · · · · · · · · · · · · · · · · · · · · · · · · ·

**Directions:** With one or more partners, choose a phrase from the list below. Write the *tempor-, chron(o)-* word and its definition on an index card. Use a dictionary to help you. Then work together to create a skit to show the meaning of the phrase. Show your skit to others without talking. See if they can guess your phrase.

> ➢ an upbeat <u>tempo</u>
>
> ➢ a <u>chronic</u> injury
>
> ➢ a <u>temporary</u> job
>
> ➢ the <u>chronology</u> of your life
>
> ➢ <u>synchronized</u> movement

Use the box below to plan your skit.

_(empty box for planning)_

# Base *later-*

## *later-* = "side"

## Standards

Uses a variety of context clues to decode unknown words

Uses combined knowledge of all letter-sound correspondences, syllabication patterns, and morphology to read accurately unfamiliar multisyllabic words in context and out of context

Reviews the key ideas expressed and draws conclusions in light of information and knowledge gained from the discussions

## Materials

- *About the Root: Base* later- (pages 104–105)

- *Divide and Conquer: Base* later- (page 106)

- *Making Connections: Write and Sketch* (page 107)

## Teaching Tips

- The Latin base *later-* means "side." Students may already know this base from sports (a *lateral* pass in football). *Later-* is used in math words that refer to the sides of a polygon. Examples include:

  - *Trilateral:* having three sides (*tri-* = "three"). A triangle is a *trilateral* polygon.

  - *Quadrilateral:* having four sides (*quadr[i]-* = "four"). The general category of *quadrilateral* polygons includes *rectangle*, *square*, *parallelogram*, and *rhombus*.

  - *Equilateral:* having sides of equal length (*equi-* = "equal").

  - *Multilateral:* having many sides (*multi-* = "many").

- Students encounter this base in social studies. (e.g., *bilateral* peace talks involve "two sides," but *unilateral* disarmament involves only "one side." *Multilateral* treaties and agreements involve many sides coming together.)

## Guided Practice

### About the Root: Base *later-*

1. Write the base *later-* on the board. Pronounce *later-* for students so they do not confuse it with the word *later*. Tell students that this base means "side." Have them work with partners to talk about and then sketch the figures described below. Invite sharing. **Note:** Remind students that *uni-* = "one," *tri-* = "three," *quadri-* = "four," and *equi-* = "equal," "same."

   - a *trilateral* figure

   - an *equilateral trilateral* figure

   - a *quadrilateral* figure

   - an *equilateral quadrilateral* figure

# Base *later-* (cont.)

**2.** Ask students to complete the About the Root pages. They can work individually or with partners. After they have finished, invite whole-group conversation. Students can share answers, talk about the text passage, or generate more words containing the root.

**3.** After students have discussed the Activate questions, invite whole-group conversation. You may wish to have students write down the shared ideas to revisit at a later time.

## Divide and Conquer: Base *later-*

**4.** As you guide students through Divide and Conquer, use questions like these to generate discussion about each of the words:

- Where is the meaning of "side" in the word _____?

- Where might you see the word _____?

- Can you think of an example of _____?

- How is the word _____ different from the word _____?

- What other words do you know that contain this root? Do these words contain the meaning of the root?

- Does the word have a suffix? If yes, what does the suffix do? Can you think of other words that have this suffix?

## Making Connections: Write and Sketch

**5.** To conclude this activity, ask students to share what they have written, item by item, and ask others if they agree or disagree and why.

### Words with *later-*

| | |
|---|---|
| bilateral | multilateral |
| collateral | quadrilateral |
| equilateral | trilateral |
| lateral | unilateral |

To print a full list of words for students, see page 155.

Name: _____ Date: _____

## About the Root:
# Base *later-*

. . . . . . . . . . . . . . . . . . . . . . . . . . . . . . . . . . . . . . . . . . . . . . . . . . . . . . . . . . . . . . . . . . . . .

## Activate

**Directions:** Think about the questions below. Discuss them with a partner.

1. How would you sketch an equilateral figure?

2. How would you sketch a quadrilateral figure?

## Respond

**Directions:** Read the passage on page 105. Then answer the questions below.

3. What would you call an equilateral polygon with three sides?

   _____

4. What is another name for an equilateral polygon with four sides?

   _____

5. Each side of an equilateral triangle measures 5 inches. What is its perimeter?

   _____

6. Each side of an equilateral square measures 10 inches. What is its perimeter?

   _____

## About the Root:
# Base *later-* (cont.)

# Equilateral Figures

In geometry, a polygon is a flat, two-dimensional shape with straight lines connected by angles (*poly-* = "many"; *gon-* = "angle"). A triangle and a square are both polygons. Each is a flat shape. Each has straight, connected lines. But a circle cannot be a polygon because its line is not straight.

*Equi-* means "equal," and *later-* means "side." From this, you can probably figure out what an *equilateral* polygon is. It is a polygon with equal sides.

It's easy to figure out the perimeter (distance around) of an equilateral polygon. All you have to do is multiply the length of one side by the number of sides.

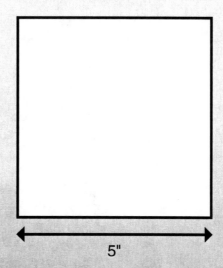

5"

Use addition to write the equation for the perimeter of this square:

_____

Use multiplication to write the equation for the perimeter of this square:

_____

Perimeter:_____

Name: _____ Date: _____

## Divide and Conquer:
# Base *later-*

**Directions:** Complete the chart below. If a word does not have a prefix, the chart is marked with X. Be sure to use *side* in your definitions. Then, write sentences on a separate sheet of paper, using two of the words from the chart. **Hint:** The suffix for all five words makes the words adjectives (describing words).

| Word | Prefix Means | Base Means | Suffix Means | Definition |
|---|---|---|---|---|
| 1. equilateral | *equi-* = equal | | | |
| 2. trilateral | *tri-* = three | | | |
| 3. quadrilateral | *quadr-* = four | | | |
| 4. lateral | X | | | |
| 5. unilateral | *uni-* = one | | | |

Name: _____ Date: _____

## Making Connections:
# Write and Sketch

. . . . . . . . . . . . . . . . . . . . . . . . . . . . . . . . . . . . . . . . . . . . . . . . . . . . . . . . . . . . . . . . . . . . . . . .

**Directions:** Work with a partner to answer the questions below.

1. Is there such a thing as a bilateral polygon? Explain.

   _____

   _____

2. Can a figure be equilateral, multilateral, and a quadrilateral all at the same time? Explain.

   _____

   _____

3. Draw a *trilateral polygon*. What is another name for this figure?

   _____

4. Lines of latitude run east to west and are parallel to the equator. Where is the "side" in *latitude*?

   _____

5. Draw a sketch to show a *lateral* pass in football.

6. Suppose two people are arguing. Explain the difference between a *unilateral* solution to the argument and a *bilateral* solution to the argument.

   _____

   _____

# Base stru-, struct-

## stru- and struct- = "build"

## Standards

Uses phonetic and structural analysis techniques, syntactic structure, and semantic context to decode unknown words

Uses common, grade-appropriate Greek and Latin affixes and roots as clues to the meaning of a word

Reviews the key ideas expressed and draws conclusions in light of information and knowledge gained from the discussions

## Materials

- *About the Root: Base* stru-, struct- (pages 110–111)

- *Divide and Conquer: Base* stru-, struct- (page 112)

- *Making Connections: Word Sort* (page 113)

## Teaching Tips

- The Latin base *stru-, struct-* means "build." Students already know several words from this base, although they may not associate them with "building." A *structure*, for example, is a "building." Students use *construction* paper in school in order to "build" projects (*con-* = "with," "together"). An *obstruction* is an obstacle, which is "built" "in the way" and blocks progress (*ob-* = "up against").

- This base appears in many words from math, technology, and engineering. Examples include:

  - *Infrastructure:* the supporting network which lies "beneath," "below" materials "built" above. The term *infrastructure* refers to bridges, highways, train tracks, sewers, and water-supply lines. The phrase "rebuilding our *infrastructure*" is frequently heard in the news.

  - *Superstructure:* the part of a building which is "built above" or over the foundation (*super-* = "over," "above").

  - *Destruction:* the demolition or taking "down" of a building (*de-* = "down," "off").

**Note:** The language of education itself is shaped by the metaphor of "building." The words *instruct, instructor,* and *instruction* all refer to the figurative idea of "building" "on" a foundation (*in-* = "in," "on," "into"). Teachers, as instructors, are special kinds of builders. We use Greek and Latin roots to "build" our students' vocabularies. We speak of "educational foundations," "building" on previous knowledge, moving to "higher" levels of understanding. We "structure" lessons that build on what our students know and use "constructive" comments to "build" new knowledge "together."

# Base stru-, struct- (cont.)

## Guided Practice

### About the Root: Base stru-, struct-

**1.** Write *stru-, struct-* on the board. Tell students that this Latin base means "build." Now, write the phrases *a construction project*, *an underground structure*, and *destruction of an old building* on the board. Tell students to work with partners to figure out where the meaning of "build" is in the underlined words. After a few minutes, invite sharing. Stress the "build" in students' responses.

**2.** Ask students to complete the About the Root pages. They can work individually or with partners. After they have finished, invite whole-group conversation. Students can share answers, talk about the text passage, or generate more words containing the root.

**3.** After students have discussed the Activate questions, invite whole-group conversation. You may wish to have students write down the shared ideas to revisit at a later time.

### Divide and Conquer: Latin Base stru-, struct-

**4.** As you guide students through Divide and Conquer, use questions like these to generate discussion about each of the words:

- Where is the meaning of "build" in the word _____?
- Where might you see the word _____?
- Can you think of an example of _____?
- How is the word _____ different from the word _____?
- What other words do you know that contain this root? Do these words contain the meaning of the root?
- Does the word have a suffix? (Students respond.) If yes, what does the suffix do? Can you think of other words that have this suffix?

### Making Connections: Word Sort

**5.** Invite discussion for the first of the word sorts. Share correct answers with the other two.

**Words with stru-, struct-**

| | |
|---|---|
| construct | instructor |
| construction | instructive |
| constructive | misconstrue |
| construe | misconstrued |
| deconstruct | obstruct |
| deconstruction | obstructed |
| destruct | reconstruct |
| destruction | reconstruction |
| destructive | restructure |
| infrastructure | structure |
| instruct | substructure |
| instruction | unobstructed |

To print a full list of words for students, see page 156.

Name: _____     Date: _____

## About the Root:
# Base stru-, struct-

. . . . . . . . . . . . . . . . . . . . . . . . . . . . . . . . . . . . . . . . . . . . . . . . . . . . . . . . . . . . .

## Activate

**Directions:** Think about the questions below. Discuss them with a partner. Use the word *build* in your answers.

1. How would you <u>construct</u> a triangle?

2. How would you <u>deconstruct</u> a triangle?

## Respond

**Directions:** Read the passage on page 111. Then answer the question below.

3. How might mathematics influence efficiency and accuracy in construction?

_____

_____

_____

_____

_____

_____

**About the Root:**
# Base *stru-, struct-* (cont.)

## Math in Construction

Suppose you were building a house. Would you need to use math? Yes! *Construction* workers use math in nearly everything they do. In fact, a brochure about math and construction from the state of Oregon says, "Math is the language of construction. It is the one 'tool' that solves nearly any problem on the job involving accuracy, efficiency, or safety."

First, how would you determine the amount of materials—boards, nails, paint—you need? You would need to know the areas and then how much of a particular material would be needed. For instance, a bedroom is 10' x 10' with 10' ceilings. You would need to calculate the square footage of the room to know how much paint to purchase.

What shape does a pointed roof resemble? That's right, a triangle. Gable roofs, which come to a point, are made of two right triangles. So if you were to build this type of roof, you would need to use geometry.

Even decorating the house when it is finished involves math. For example, you may want to hang three pictures on a wall in a triangular shape.

If you think more about it, you can probably think of many other examples for using math in construction. Perhaps math really *is* the language of construction.

http://ccwd.oregon.gov/dwu/edocs/IncreaseYourSkills.pdf

Name: _____     Date: _____

## Divide and Conquer:
## Base *stru-, struct-*

**Directions:** Complete the chart below. If a word does not have a prefix or a suffix, the chart is marked with X. Be sure to use *build* in your definitions. Then, write sentences on a separate sheet of paper, using two of the words from the chart. **Hint:** One word has a suffix that makes the word an adjective (a describing word). Three words have the same suffix. The suffix makes the words nouns (things or objects).

| Word | Prefix Means | Base Word | Suffix Means | Definition |
|------|-------------|-----------|--------------|------------|
| 1. infrastructure | *infra-* = beneath, below | | | |
| 2. construct | *con-* = with, together | | X | |
| 3. superstructure | *super-* = over, above | | | |
| 4. structure | X | | | |
| 5. destructive | *de-* = down, off | | | |

Name: _____ Date: _____

## Making Connections:
# Word Sort

**Directions:** Work with a partner. Put the words on the charts where they belong.

**Word Bank**

| construct | constructor | instruct | instructor | reconstructed |
| construction | deconstruction | instruction | obstruction | structure |

| Person | Thing | Action |
|---|---|---|
| Constructor | Structure | reconstructed |
| instructor | | instruction |
| | | obstruction |
| | | construction |
| | | deconstruction |

| Has No Prefix | Has One Prefix | Has More Than One Prefix |
|---|---|---|
| Structure | Construct | reconstructed |
| | construction | deconstruction |
| | Constructor | |
| | instruct | |
| | instruction | |
| | instructor | |
| | Obstruction | |

| Has a Suffix | Does Not Have a Suffix |
|---|---|
| instruction | Construct |
| construction | instruct |
| construction | structure |
| instructor | |
| obstruction | |
| reconstructed | |
| deconstruction | |
| constructer | |

Name: _____   Date: _____

## Unit III Review:
# Magic Square

**Directions:** Match each word on the left to the sentence it completes on the right. Then put the numbers and the words onto the chart on page 115 where they belong.

| | | |
|---|---|---|
| _____ **A.** circumference | **1.** | The _____ of a rectangle is two times its height added to two times its width. |
| _____ **B.** chronology | **2.** | _____ diseases can be very difficult for people. |
| _____ **C.** chronic | **3.** | I kept a _____ of our move from the moment we decided to move until the moment we got settled in our new home. |
| _____ **D.** diameter | **4.** | We had a flood at our school, so we are _____ attending classes in an empty factory. |
| _____ **E.** quadrilaterals | **5.** | Squares, rhombuses, and other parallelograms are all _____. |
| _____ **F.** construct | **6.** | A square is always an _____ figure. |
| _____ **G.** destruction | **7.** | Triangles, squares, and hexagons are all _____ because they have multiple sides. |
| _____ **H.** instructor | **8.** | Our math _____ is a great teacher! |
| _____ **I.** construction | **9.** | Using math in _____ enhances efficiency and accuracy. |
| _____ **J.** equilateral | **10.** | To _____ an equilateral triangle, you need 3 lines of equal length. |
| _____ **K.** multilateral | **11.** | Math is used more in the construction of a building than in its _____. |
| _____ **L.** diagonal | **12.** | The _____ of a square crosses from the lower right angle to the upper left angle. |
| _____ **M.** temporarily | **13.** | The _____ of a circle is twice its radius. |
| _____ **N.** circle | **14.** | _____ or sketches often help us figure out math problems. |
| _____ **O.** diagrams | **15.** | A _____ and an ellipse are both curved shapes. |
| _____ **P.** perimeter | **16.** | The _____ of a circle is the product of its diameter and pi. |

Name: _____  Date: _____

## Unit III Review:
# Magic Square

**Directions:** Use the words and sentences on page 114 to put the numbers onto the chart below where they belong. Check your answers. If you are correct, all rows and columns will add up to the same "magic" number.

| | | | |
|---|---|---|---|
| A: | B: | C: | D: |
| E: | F: | G: | H: |
| I: | J: | K: | L: |
| M: | N: | O: | P: |

**Magic Number:**

_____

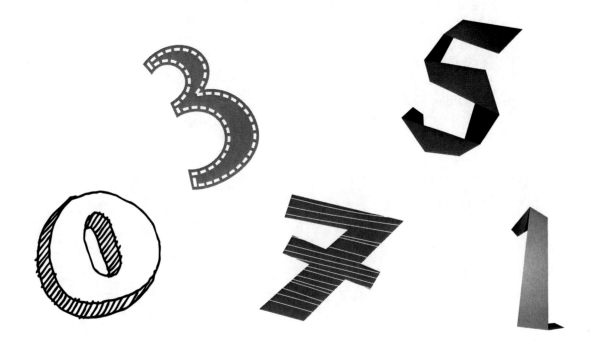

# Answer Key

## Unit I: Lesson 1–Directional Prefix *a-, ab-, abs-*

**About the Root: Directional Prefix *a-, ab-, abs-* (page 22)**

1–3. Students' answers will vary.

**Divide and Conquer: Directional Prefixes *a-, ab-,* and *abs-* (page 24)**

Students' answers for the "definition" section may vary; accept a range of answers.

1. abstain = away or from; to keep away from certain foods or activities (e.g., *abstain* from dairy products); to hold one's vote back and not cast it or give it "away" (e.g., to *abstain* from voting yes or no; such a non-vote is called an *abstention*)

2. abrupt = away or from; suddenly breaking away from an ongoing activity (e.g., coming to an *abrupt* halt); having curt manners and being short with people; suddenly breaking off from conversation and turning away (e.g., an *abrupt* comment)

3. avert = away or from; to prevent something from happening, to avoid (e.g., to *avert* disaster, to *avert* a strike); to turn away (e.g., to *avert* one's eyes and look away)

4. abduct = away or from; to forcibly lead away from the premises; to kidnap (e.g., to *abduct* a child from the playground)

5. abnormal = away or from; deviating from the norm; unusual or irregular (e.g., *abnormally* high temperatures, an *abnormal* reaction, an *abnormal* rash)

**Making Connections: Word Fun (page 25)**

1–5. Students' answers will vary.

## Unit I: Lesson 2–Directional Prefix *ad-*

**About the Root: Directional Prefix *ad-* (page 28)**

1–4. Students' answers will vary.

**Divide and Conquer: Directional Prefix *ad-* (page 30)**

Students' answers for the "definition" section may vary; accept a range of answers.

1. adapt = to, toward, or add to; to make changes or adjustments "to" something for a better fit (e.g., to *adapt* to your surroundings; to make *adaptations* to something for a better fit; an *adapter* "fits" an electrical appliance "to" the current)

2. admonish = to, toward, or add to; to give a warning "to" someone; to give a reminder or stern advice (e.g., to *admonish* a student for being tardy; such a word of warning is an *admonition*)

3. adhere = to, toward, or add to; to stick to (e.g., *adhesive* tape *adheres* to the surface); to follow closely and "stick to" rules or requirements (e.g., to *adhere* to the Constitution; to *adhere* closely to the directions)

4. advent = to, toward, or add to; the onset or arrival of a person or event (e.g., the *advent* of the automobile quickened the pace of American life); written with an upper case *A*, *Advent* is the 40-day period of preparation for Christmas

5. adversary = to, toward, or add to; a foe, rival or opponent; one who turns "to," "toward" a rival of unfriendly competition; the adjectival form of this noun is *adversarial*, as in "an adversarial relationship"

**Making Connections: Word Sort (page 31)**

| 2 Syllables | 3 Syllables | 4 or More Syllables |
|---|---|---|
| adapt | adaptive | additional |
| address | addendum | adversary |
| advent | adhesion | |
| adhere | adjective | |
| | admonish | |

# Answer Key *(cont.)*

| Is or Could Describe a Person | Is Not/Could Not Describe a Person |
|---|---|
| adaptive, additional, adversary | All possible answers include: adapt, addendum, address, advent, adhesion, adhere, adjective, admonish |

| Describes An Action | Does Not Describe An Action |
|---|---|
| adapt, address, adhere, admonish | All possible answers include: adaptive, addendum, advent, adhesion, additional, adjective, adversary (depending on rationale *address* could be here too) |

## Unit I: Lesson 3—Base *sed-, sid-, sess-*

### About the Root: Base *sed-, sid-, sess-* (page 34)

1–5. Students' answers will vary.

### Divide and Conquer: Base *sed-, sid-, sess-* (page 36)

Students' answers for the "definition" section may vary; accept a range of answers.

1. residence = sit or settle; a house or dwelling in which one "sits back," as opposed to a place of work; a *residential* area consists of houses, unlike industrial or commercial areas in which jobs are performed

2. president = sit or settle; a chief executive officer, usually elected; one who *presides* over a corporation, government, etc. (a *president* "sits before" others at a meeting in a position of authority and leadership)

3. subside = sit or settle; to settle down at a lower level of intensity (e.g., a headache may *subside*; tensions may *subside*, heavy rains eventually *subside*)

4. sedentary = sit or settle; performed from a seated position; not requiring physical exertion (e.g., a *sedentary* job is a "desk job"; a *sedentary* lifestyle does not include physical exercise)

5. session = sit or settle; an official meeting of a group that sits to conduct its work (e.g., court is now in *session*, class is now in *session*, a *session* of Congress)

### Making Connections: Magic Square (page 37)

**A.** 5    **B.** 7    **C.** 3

**D.** 9    **E.** 2    **F.** 4

**G.** 1    **H.** 6    **I.** 8

**Magic Number:** 15

## Unit I:—Lesson 4—Base *duc-, duct-*

### About the Root: Base *duc-, duct-* (page 40)

1–3. Students' answers will vary.

### Divide and Conquer: Base *duc-, duct-* (page 42)

Students' answers for the "definition" section may vary; accept a range of answers.

1. reduce = lead; to make smaller in size or fewer in quantity; to "lead back" to an earlier and smaller state (e.g., people on a weight *reduction* program try to get their weight back to a lower number)

2. educate = lead; originally, to raise a child by "leading" it "out of" childhood through training, instruction, and discipline; to lead or guide a person by teaching

3. introduce = lead; to "lead" or "bring in" especially for the first time

4. conductor = lead; one who leads together the musicians of an orchestra; on a train, the person responsible for "leading together" all other workers to guarantee a coordinated and smooth operation; our *conduct* is the manner in which we "lead" ourselves when we are "with" others

# Answer Key (cont.)

5. inductee = lead; a person who has been led into any official group, such as the Army, a Hall of Fame, or an honorary society

6. productive = lead; bringing about results; "leading" a process "forward," "ahead" so that it moves toward the desired goal or end

## Making Connections: Authors and Illustrators (page 43)

Students' answers will vary.

## Unit I: Lesson 5–Suffixes -cracy and -crat

### About the Root: Suffixes -cracy and -crat (page 46)

1–4. Students' answers will vary.

### Divide and Conquer: Suffixes -cracy and -crat (page 48)

Students' answers for the "definition" section may vary; accept a range of answers.

1. democracy = rule by, ruler, or one who believes in rule; rule or government of, by, and for the people (note: the Greek base *dem[o]-* refers to collective people in communities, as opposed to individuals acting on their own personal behalf)

2. aristocrat = rule by, ruler, or one who believes in rule; one who believes in rule or government by the best people (the best people are self-defined as owners of land and inherited wealth; the terms *aristocracy* and *aristocrat* are based in a class system)

3. plutocrat = rule by, ruler, or one who believes in rule; one who believes in rule or government by the wealthy (a *plutocrat* believes that wealth, including newly acquired money and profits earned in business, is the major criterion of power; an *aristocrat*, by contrast, believes that the wealth must be inherited from an old family of landholders)

4. autocrat = rule by, ruler, or one who believes in rule; a "self ruler," one who sets his own rules and governs by them (*autocrats* are often likened to despots and tyrants)

5. theocracy = rule by, ruler, or one who believes in rule; rule by God (i.e., by the state religion and its commandments; in a *theocracy*, violations of religious rules can be treated as if they were crimes against the state)

## Making Connections: Word Sort (page 49)

| Types of Organization or Government | Person | Adjective (Describing Word) |
|---|---|---|
| aristocracy | aristocrat | aristocratic |
| autocracy | autocrat | autocratic |
| bureaucracy | bureaucrat | bureaucratic |
| technocracy | technocrat | technocratic |

## Unit I Review

### Crossword Puzzle (page 50–51)

| Across | Down |
|---|---|
| 3. abdication | 1. abstract |
| 7. supersede | 2. abduction |
| 9. bureaucrat | 3. abolished |
| 11. aqueducts | 4. address |
| | 5. assessor |
| | 6. democrat |
| | 8. aristocracy |
| | 10. addendum |

## Unit II: Lesson 1–Base center-, centr(i)-

### About the Root: Base center-, centr(i)- (page 54)

1–4. Students' answers will vary.

### Divide and Conquer: Base center-, centr(i)- (page 56)

Students' answers for the "definition" section may vary; accept a range of answers.

1. geocentric = center; earth-centered (e.g., the *geocentric* orbit of the moon around Earth)

# Answer Key *(cont.)*

2. heliocentric = center; sun-centered (e.g., the Earth's orbit around the sun)

3. hypocenter = center; the center point, below the earth's surface, at which an earthquake originates

4. concentric = center; having a shared center with another circle or ring (e.g., *concentric* circles never intersect, but *eccentric* circles do)

5. epicenter = center; the center of the earth's surface directly above the hypocenter of an earthquake

## Making Connections: Magic Square (page 57)

| | | | | |
|---|---|---|---|---|
| **A.** 9 | **C.** 7 | **E.** 6 | **G.** 5 | **I.** 3 |
| **B.** 2 | **D.** 4 | **F.** 8 | **H.** 10 | **J.** 1 |

**Magic Number:** 18

## Unit II: Lesson 2–Base *audi-, audit-*

### About the Root: Base *audi-, audit-* (page 60)

**1–4.** Students' answers will vary.

### Divide and Conquer: Base *audi-, audit-* (page 62)

Students' answers for the "definition" section may vary; accept a range of answers.

1. audible = hear or listen; able to be heard (e.g., *audible* whispers, *audible* sound patterns)

2. audiophile = hear or listen; one who loves to listen, especially to recorded music; a listening enthusiast who pays close attention to the quality and precision of sound recordings

3. audiometer = hear or listen; a device that measures hearing ability

4. audition = hear or listen; a tryout in which a contestant is heard by judges; also, as a verb, to try out for a role or for a place in a performing group

5. auditory = hear or listen; pertaining to the ear and hearing (such as *auditory* nerves, the *auditory* system, and *auditory* specialists)

**6–7.** Students' answers will vary.

## Making Connections: Scramble (page 63)

| | |
|---|---|
| **1.** audiovisual | **6.** audiometer |
| **2.** audience | **7.** auditory |
| **3.** inaudible | **8.** audio-lingual |
| **4.** audible; auditorium | **9.** Answers will vary. |
| **5.** audiologist | **10.** Answers will vary. |

## Unit II: Lesson 3–Base *pon-, pos-, posit-*

### About the Root: Base *pon-, pos-, posit-* (page 66)

**1–3.** Students' answers will vary.

### Divide and Conquer: Base *pon-, pos-, posit-* (page 68)

Students' answers for the "definition" section may vary; accept a range of answers.

1. compost = place or put; a pile of organic matter that has been put together from leaves, grass, vegetable peelings, etc.

2. deposit = place or put; to put something down (e.g., a river *deposits* sediment; we *deposit* money when we put it down on a banker's counter; fluvial *deposits* are found at the bottom of river beds)

3. position = place or put; the act of placing or arranging

4. expose = place or put; to put something out in the open where it is subject to harm or damage by the elements, etc. (e.g., frostbite is caused by *exposure* of the extremities to extreme cold)

5. opponent = place or put; a rival or challenger who puts himself or herself in the way, who resists and obstructs (e.g., *proponents* of a cause "put" an idea "forward," but *opponents* challenge and resist such proposals)

6. composite = place or put; made up of different parts or substances which have been put together to form a whole; a police composite is a sketch of a suspect that has been put together from various details described by a witness

# Answer Key (cont.)

## Making Connections: Guess the Word (page 69)

1. compose
2. decompose
3. decomposition
4. deposit
5. compost
6. dispose
7. oppose
8. positive
9. exposure
10. composition

## Unit II: Lesson 4—Bases *aqua-* and *hydr(o)-*

### About the Root: Bases *aqua-* and *hydr(o)-* (page 72)

1–2. Students' answers will vary.

### Divide and Conquer: Bases *aqua-* and *hydr(o)-* (page 74)

Students' answers for the "definition" section may vary; accept a range of answers.

1. aqueous = water; watery, consisting of water (e.g., an *aqueous* solution, *aqueous* membranes)

2. hydroplane = water; as a noun; a plane that can land on and take off from water (a *hydrofoil*); as a verb, to skid over a wet surface (e.g., to *hydroplane* while driving a car at high speed and hitting a patch of water on the road)

3. hydrophobia = water; fear of water; technical name for rabies, which is characterized by an animal's frothing mouth, which indicates *dehydration*)

4. aquatic = water; thriving and growing in water (e.g., *aquatic* plants, *aquatic* animals); performed in water (e.g., *aquatic* sports)

5. hydrogen = water; an element which, when combined with oxygen, produces water

### Making Connections: Drawing and Acting (page 75)

Students' answers will vary.

## Unit II: Lesson 5—Bases *dent-* and *odont-*

### About the Root: Bases *dent-* and *odont-* (page 78)

1–4. Students' answers will vary.

### Divide and Conquer: Bases *dent-* and *odont-* (page 80)

Students' answers for the "definition" section may vary; accept a range of answers.

1. exodontist = teeth; a person who takes out teeth; a dental surgeon

2. trident = teeth; a spear or harpoon with three prongs or "teeth"; also, a brand of chewing gum that claims not to stick to dental work

3. periodontist = teeth; a person who specializes in the membranes around the teeth (i.e., the gums)

4. orthodontics = teeth; the branch of medicine dealing with the straightening of teeth

5. dentition = teeth; the formation of teeth (e.g., the cutting of teeth by young children)

### Making Connections: Word Sort (page 81)

| Contains *dent-* | | Contains *odont-* |
|---|---|---|
| dental | dentures | mastodon |
| dentifrice | indent | orthodontics |
| dentist | trident | orthodontist |
| | | periodontics |

| Is or Was Alive | Is Not Alive | |
|---|---|---|
| dentist | dental | orthodontics |
| orthodontist | dentifrice | periodontics |
| mastodon | dentures | trident |
| | indent | |

| Beginning of Word | Middle of Word | End of Word |
|---|---|---|
| dental | orthodontics | indent |
| dentifrice | orthodontist | mastodon |
| dentist | periodontics | trident |
| dentures | | |

# Answer Key *(cont.)*

## Unit II Review

### Crossword Puzzle (pages 82–83)

| Across | Down |
|---|---|
| 4. hydrated | 1. audiometer |
| 5. exposed | 2. audiologist |
| 6. dental | 3. compost |
| 10. inaudible | 4. hydrogen |
| 11. centrifuge | 6. dentures |
| 12. deposits | 7. aquarium |
| | 8. epicenter |
| | 9. centrist |

## Unit III: Lesson 1—Prefix *dia-*

### About the Root: Prefix *dia-* (page 86)

1–3. Students' answers will vary.

### Divide and Conquer: Prefix *dia-* (page 88)

Students' answers for the "definition" section may vary; accept a range of answers.

1. diameter = through, across, or thorough; the line of measurement that cuts through or across a circle's center. When people are *diametrically* opposed, their views are at the furthest degree possible from one another: they are as far apart as the two points of a circle's *diameter*

2. diagnosis = through, across, or thorough; a thorough explanation or reading of the symptoms of a disease (*diagnostic* tests aim for a thorough evaluation of a problem, of a student's mastery of the subject matter, etc.)

3. diagram = through, across, or thorough; a sketch or outline consisting of lines drawn across the page

4. diagonal = through, across, or thorough; a line cutting across a polygon and joining nonadjacent angles; a slanted line inside a rectangle connecting opposite corners

5. dialogue = through, across, or thorough; a conversation in which speakers talk "through" a problem at great length

### Making Connections: Sketch to Stretch (page 89)

Students' answers will vary.

## Unit III: Lesson 2—Prefixes *peri-*, *circum-*, and *circu-*

### About the Root: Prefixes *peri-*, *circum-*, and *circu-* (page 92)

1–3. Students' answers will vary.

### Divide and Conquer: Prefixes *peri-*, *circum-*, and *circu-* (page 94)

Students' answers for the "definition" section may vary; accept a range of answers.

1. perimeter = around; the measurement around a polygon, computed by adding together the length of all its sides

2. circumference = around; the measurement around a circle, computed by multiplying the diameter by pi *(c = pi x d)*

3. circuitous = around; moving in a roundabout manner, indirect

4. periscope = around; a viewing device enabling the viewer to look around corners, over the sea's surface, etc.

5. circumnavigate = around; to sail around the globe; to sail around any land mass (such as an island or peninsula)

# Answer Key (cont.)

## Making Connections: Scramble (page 95)

1. circumnavigated
2. semicircle
3. perimeter
4. periscope
5. circular
6. peripheral
7. circumference
8. circulatory
9. encircle
10. periodicals

## Unit III: Lesson 3—Bases *tempor-* and *chron(o)-*

### About the Root: Bases *tempor-* and *chron(o)-* (page 98)

1–4. Students' answers will vary.

### Divide and Conquer: Bases *tempor-* and *chron(o)-* (page 100)

Students' answers for the "definition" section may vary; accept a range of answers.

1. contemporary = time; occurring at the same time with another; modern and keeping up with the times (as in *contemporary* ideas); one's age-mate

2. chronic = time; long-lasting, enduring over time (as in a *chronic* medical condition; *chronic* pain, etc.)

3. temporary = time; not permanent (as in a *temporary* solution to a problem); intended to last "for the time being" (as in a *temporary* appointment of an official)

4. synchronize = time; to set the "time together," to set two or more watches at precisely the same time; to perform a maneuver or feat by many people moving at precisely the same time (as in *synchronized* swimming)

5. chronicles = time; historical records of events as they occur over time, usually on a year-by-year basis (also, to *chronicle* an event means to monitor it closely over time and keep records, paying attention to the *chronological* order in which they take place)

### Making Connections: Wordless Skits (page 101)

Students' answers will vary.

## Unit III: Lesson 4—Base *later-*

### About the Root: Base *later-* (page 104)

1–2. Students' answers will vary.

3. triangle
4. square
5. 15 inches
6. 40 inches

### Divide and Conquer: Base *later-* (page 106)

Students' answers for the "definition" section may vary; accept a range of answers.

1. equilateral = side; equal-sided; having sides of equal length (*equilateral* polygons are also equiangular)

2. trilateral = side; three-sided (a triangle is a *trilateral* polygon; international peace talks involving three sides are *trilateral* negotiations)

3. quadrilateral = side; four-sided (all quadrangles are also *quadrilateral*, such as rectangle, square, parallelogram, and rhombus)

4. lateral = side; thrown to the side; a sideways pass in sports; also, located on the side of a body (e.g., *lateral* muscles, the *lateral* fins of fish, etc.)

5. unilateral = side; one-sided; addressing only one side of an issue; describing a decision made by only one side of multiple parties

### Making Connections: Write and Sketch (page 107)

1. No; lines need to connect, and the only way that could happen with 2 lines is if they're on top of one another

2. Yes, a square has equal sides, many sides, and four sides

3. Triangle

4. Students' answers will vary.

5. Ball should be going sideways, not forward or backward

6. Unilateral— one side benefits from the solution; bilateral—both sides agree on solution

# Answer Key (cont.)

## Unit III: Lesson 5–Base *stru-, struct-*

### About the Root: Base stru-, *struct-* (page 110)

**1–3.** Students' answers will vary.

### Divide and Conquer: Base *stru-, struct-* (page 112)

Students' answers for the "definition" section may vary; accept a range of answers.

1. infrastructure = build; the network of support systems for roads and buildings; the "underlying construction" of support for roads, railways, etc.

2. construct = build; to build; to put together various materials and build something out of them (e.g., *constructive* criticism aims to build improvement, *constructive* comments build up the project at hand)

3. superstructure = build; the part of a building erected on top of the foundation

4. structure = build; any building; also, the system or manner in which complex structures are put together (e.g., the *structure* of an atom, the *structure* of a play, bone *structure*)

5. destructive = build; causing harm; having the effect of destroying things and tearing them down (this word is an antonym of *constructive*, which describes the creative process of building)

## Making Connections: Word Sort (page 113)

| Person | Thing | Action |
|---|---|---|
| instructor constructor | construction deconstruction instruction structure obstruction | construct instruct reconstructed |

| Has No Prefix | Has One Prefix | Has More Than One Prefix |
|---|---|---|
| structure | construct construction instruct instructor instruction obstruction constructor | deconstruction reconstructed |

| Has a Suffix | Does Not Have a Suffix | |
|---|---|---|
| construction deconstruction instructor instruction structure reconstructed obstruction constructor | construct instruct | |

## Unit III Review

### Magic Square (page 114–115)

**A.** 16　**B.** 3　**C.** 2　**D.** 13

**E.** 5　**F.** 10　**G.** 11　**H.** 8

**I.** 9　**J.** 6　**K.** 7　**L.** 12

**M.** 4　**N.** 15　**O.** 14　**P.** 1

**Magic Number:** 34

# References Cited

Baumann, James, Elizabeth C. Carr-Edwards, George Font, Cathleen A. Tereshinski, Edward J. Kame'enui, and Stephen Olejnik. "Teaching Morphemic and Contextual Analysis to Fifth-Grade Students." *Reading Research Quarterly* 37 (2002): 150–176.

Baumann, James F., George Font, Elizabeth C. Edwards, and Eileen Boland. "Strategies for Teaching Middle-Grade Students to Use Word-Part and Context Clues to Expand Reading Vocabulary." In *Teaching and Learning Vocabulary: Bringing Research to Practice*, edited by Elfrieda H. Hiebert and Michael L. Kamil, 179–205. Mahwah, NJ: Erlbaum, 2005.

Bear, Donald, Marcia Invernizzi, Shane Templeton, and Francine R. Johnston. *Words Their Way (5th Edition)*. Upper Saddle River, NJ: Prentice Hall, 2011.

Beck, Isabel L., Margaret G. McKeown, and Linda Kucan. *Bringing Words to Life: Robust Vocabulary Instruction*. New York: Guilford, 2002.

Beck, Isabel, Charles A. Perfetti, and Margaret G. McKeown. "Effects of Long-Term Vocabulary Instruction on Lexical Access and Reading Comprehension." *Journal of Educational Psychology* 74 (1982): 506–521.

Biemiller, Andrew. "Implications for Choosing Words for Primary Grade Vocabulary." In *Teaching and Learning Vocabulary: Bringing Research to Practice*, edited by by Elfrieda H. Hiebert and Michael L. Kamil, 223–242. Mahwah, NJ: Erlbaum, 2005.

Biemiller, Andrew, and Naomi Slonim. "Estimating Root Word Vocabulary Growth in Normative and Advantaged Populations: Evidence for a Common Sequence of Vocabulary Acquisition." *Journal of Educational Psychology* 93 (2001): 498–520.

Blachowicz, Camille, and Peter Fisher. *Teaching Vocabulary in All Classrooms (3rd Edition)*. Upper Saddle River, NJ: Pearson/Merrill/Prentice Hall, 2006.

Blachowicz, Camille, Peter Fisher, Donna Ogle, and Susan Watts-Taffe. "Vocabulary: Questions from the Classroom." *Reading Research Quarterly* 41 (2006): 524–538.

Carlisle, Joanne F. "Awareness of the Structure and Meaning of Morphologically Complex Words: Impact on Reading." *Reading and Writing: An Interdisciplinary Journal* 12 (2000): 169–190.

———. "Effects of Instruction in Morphological Awareness on Literacy Achievement: An Integrative Review." *Reading Research Quarterly* 45 (2010): 464–487.

Chandler, Richard E., and Kessel Schwartz. *A New History of Spanish Literature*. Baton Rouge, LA: LSU Press, 1961/1991.

Cunningham, Patricia M. *Phonics They Use: Words for Reading and Writing*. New York: Longman, 2004.

# References Cited (cont.)

Graves, M.F., and S.M. Watts-Taffe. "The Place of Word Consciousness in a Research-Based Vocabulary Program." In *What Research Has to Say About Reading Instruction*, edited by Alan E. Farstrup and S. Jay Samuels, 140–165. Newark, DE: International Reading Association, 2002.

Harmon, Janis M., Wanda B. Hedrick, and Karen D. Wood. "Research on Vocabulary Instruction in the Content Areas: Implications for Struggling Readers." *Reading & Writing Quarterly* 21 (2005): 261–280.

Kame'enui, Edward J., Douglas W. Carnine, and Roger Freschi. "Effects of Text Construction and Instructional Procedures for Teaching Word Meanings on Comprehension and Recall." *Reading Research Quarterly* 17 (1982): 367–388.

Kieffer, Michael, and Nonie K. Lesaux. "Breaking Down Words to Build Meaning: Morphology, Vocabulary, and Reading Comprehension in the Urban Classroom." *The Reading Teacher* 61 (2007): 134–144.

Lehr, Fran, Jean Osborn, and Elfrieda H. Hiebert. "Research-Based Practices in Early Reading Series: A Focus on Vocabulary." 2004. http://www.eric.ed.gov/?id=ED483190.

Mountain, Lee. "ROOTing Out Meaning: More Morphemic Analysis for Primary Pupils." *The Reading Teacher* 58 (2005): 742–749.

Nagy, William, Richard C. Anderson, Marlene Schommer, Judith Ann Scott, and Anne C. Stallman. "Morphological Families in the Internal Lexicon." *Reading Research Quarterly* 24 (1989): 262–282.

Nagy, William, and Judith Ann Scott. "Vocabulary Processes." In *Handbook of Reading Research*, Vol. III, edited by Michael L. Kamil, Peter B. Mosenthal, P. David Pearson, and Rebecca Barr, 269–284. Mahwah, NJ: Erlbaum, 2000.

Porter-Collier, I.M. "Teaching Vocabulary Through the Roots Approach in order to Increase Comprehension and Metacognition." Unpublished masters degree project. Akron OH: University of Akron, 2010.

Rasinski, Timothy, and Nancy Padak. *From Phonics to Fluency (3rd Edition)*. New York: Longman, 2013.

Rasinski, Timothy, Nancy Padak, Evangeline Newton, and Rick M. Newton. *Greek and Latin Roots: Keys to Building Vocabulary*. Huntington Beach, CA: Shell Educational Publishing, 2008.

Stahl, Steven A., and Marilyn M. Fairbanks. "The Effects of Vocabulary Instruction: A Model-Based Meta-Analysis." *Review of Educational Research* 56 (1986): 72–110.

# Additional Practice Activities

Use the activities below to provide extra practice, to share with parents, or to differentiate instruction.

## Card Games

The following card games can offer practice with roots:

### Concentration (or Memory)

Select eight to ten words containing a root or base. Make double sets of word cards for each (or put the word and its definition on separate cards). Shuffle the cards and put them facedown on a table. Players take turns trying to make matches. The player with the most cards wins the game.

### Go Fish

Select four to six bases. For each, create a set of four words (see Appendix E for related words). Students use these to play "Go Fish."

### Word War

Provide words containing several roots and related terms written on cards. Play the card game "War" with them. Each player turns up a card. The person whose card a) comes first in alphabetical order, b) has more letters, or c) has more syllables wins the round as long as he or she can say both words and their meanings. If the words are similar, players draw again and the same rules as before apply. The player who wins this "war" takes all of the cards. A player who gets all of his or her partner's cards wins the game.

## Word Games

The following word games can offer practice with roots:

### List-Group-Label or Word Webs

Provide a root. Ask students to brainstorm words containing the root. Write these on the board or chart paper. Then ask small groups to work with the words by:

* listing related terms and providing labels for them.

* developing a graphic, such as a web, that shows how the words are related.

# Additional Practice Activities *(cont.)*

## Root Word Riddles

Who doesn't enjoy the brain-teasing process of trying to solve a riddle? This strategy invites students to create and guess riddles with words from the same base. Give pairs of students a list of words that contain the targeted base. Each pair's job is to devise riddles for other students to solve. (You may want to model riddle creation for students.) Example:

**invisible**

1. I have four syllables.

2. I have two word parts.

3. One part means "not."

4. The other part means "see."

5. I mean "not perceptible to the human eye."

What am I?

## Sketch to Stretch

Provide words written on slips of paper and distribute them to students. Ask students to sketch something that reveals the word meaning. Then have them share these with others, who try to guess what their classmates have drawn.

## Wordo

This vocabulary version of Bingo is a wonderful way for students to play with new words they are learning. List 24 words containing the targeted root(s) on the board. Duplicate a Wordo card found on pages 129–130 and on the Digital Resource CD (filename: 4x4wordomatrix.pdf and 5x5wordomatrix.pdf) for each student. Ask each student to choose a free box and mark it. Then have them write one of the words from the board in each of the remaining boxes. Students choose whatever box they wish for each word.

Now call a clue for each word: the definition, a synonym, an antonym, or a sentence with the target word deleted. Students figure out the correct target word and then draw an *X* through it. (If you want to clear the sheets and play again, use small scraps of paper or other small items to mark the squares.) When a student has *X*s or markers in a row, a column, a diagonal, or four corners, he or she can call out "Wordo!"

# Additional Practice Activities (cont.)

## Word Skits

List eight to ten words containing the targeted root(s) on the board. Divide students into teams of three to four. Each team chooses one word and writes its definition on an index card. Working together, they create a skit or situation that shows the meaning of the word. The skit is performed without words. Classmates try to guess the word being shown. Once the word is correctly identified, the definition is read out loud.

## Word Sorts

Select about ten words containing the targeted root(s). Put the words on individual cards or slips of paper. (If you are introducing Word Sorts to students, you may also want to put the words on a blank transparency and cut them apart so that you can demonstrate the process of sorting the words.)

Provide one set of word cards to each pair of students. Ask students to group the words. Remind them that they will be asked to explain their groupings. Some criteria for grouping include:

**a.** presence/absence of a prefix or suffix

**b.** number of syllables

**c.** presence/absence of a long-vowel sound (in general, or a particular long-vowel sound)

After a few minutes, invite students to tell about one of their groups, both the words contained in it and the reason for putting them together. If time permits, ask students to sort the same set of words repeatedly (e.g., by presence/absence of word part, or by number of syllables). Each sort provides students another opportunity to think about both the words and their component parts.

## Word Spokes

Duplicate a Word Spokes chart for each student or pair of students found on page 131 and on the Digital Resource CD (filename: wordspokeschart.pdf). Put the targeted root on the board. Have students put the targeted root in the center. Ask students to identify enough words containing the root to complete the chart. You may want to ask students to add sentences or illustrations of selected words as well. Conclude the activity with sharing.

## Be the Bard

Have students combine the roots covered in the book in different ways to create new words (e.g., *hemiport, motiport*), in much the same way that Shakespeare created new words such as *bedroom* and *premeditated*.

# 4 x 4 Wordo Matrix

| | | | |
|---|---|---|---|
| | | | |
| | | | |
| | | | |
| | | | |

# 5 x 5 Wordo Matrix

| | | | | |
|---|---|---|---|---|
| | | | | |
| | | | | |
| | | | | |
| | | | | |
| | | | | |

# Word Spokes Chart

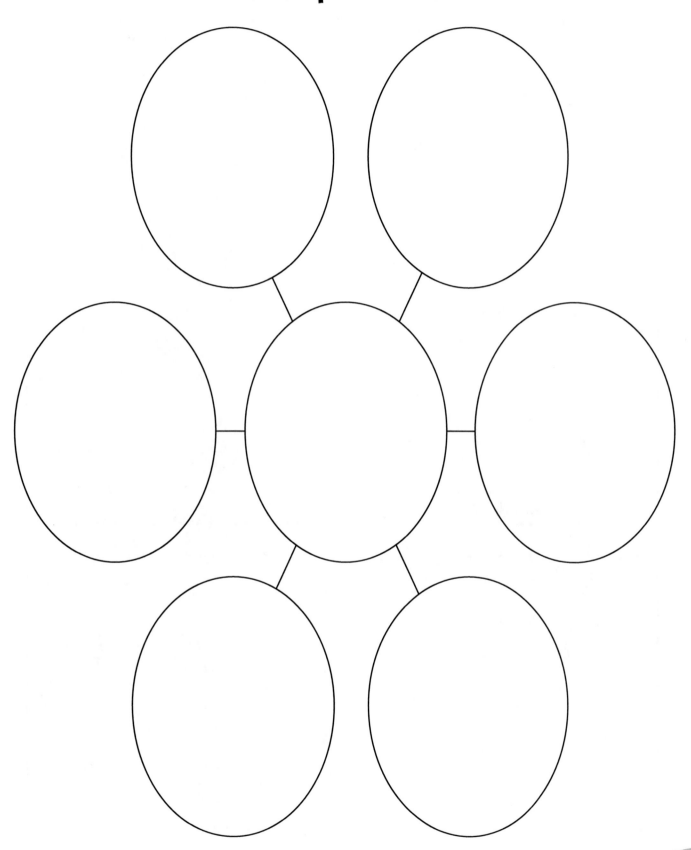

Name: _____    Date: _____

## Unit I–Lesson 1:
# Directional Prefix a-, ab-, abs-

**Directions:** The words on the chart have the prefix *a-*, *ab-*, *abs-*, which means "away," "from." Write the letter from the Definition Bank for the correct word.

| Word | Prefix Means | Base Means | Definition |
|------|-------------|------------|------------|
| 1. abstain | | *tain-* = hold | |
| 2. abrupt | | *rupt-* = break | |
| 3. avert | | *vert-* = turn | |
| 4. abduct | | *duct-* = lead | |
| 5. abnormal | | *norm-* = norm | |

**Definition Bank**

A. coming to a sudden end; unexpected

B. irregular or unusual

C. to avoid or prevent from happening

D. to kidnap

E. to withhold one's vote; to keep away from an activity

Name: _____ Date: _____

# Directional Prefix ad-

**Directions:** The words on the chart have the prefix *ad-*, which means "to," "toward," or "add to." Write the letter from the Definition Bank for the correct word.

| Word | Prefix Means | Base Means | Definition |
|---|---|---|---|
| 1.  adapt |  | *apt-* = fit |  |
| 2.  admonish |  | *mon-* = warn |  |
| 3.  adhere |  | *her-* = stick, cling |  |
| 4.  advent |  | *vent-* = come |  |
| 5.  adversary |  | *vers-* = turn |  |

**Definition Bank**

A.  to chastise; to express disapproval

B.  foe, rival, opponent

C.  to adjust or modify

D.  arrival or onset; also, for Christians, the 40-day period before Christmas

E.  to hold fast to

Name: _____ Date: _____

## Unit I–Lesson 3:
# Base *sed-*, *sid-*, *sess-*

**Directions:** The words on the chart have the base *sed-*, *sid-*, *sess-*, which means "sit" or "settle." (*X* means that the word has no prefix.) Write the letter from the Definition Bank for the correct word.

| Word | Prefix Means | Base Means | Definition |
|---|---|---|---|
| 1.  residence | *re-* = back, again | | |
| 2.  president | *pre-* = before, in front of | | |
| 3.  subside | *sub-* = below, under | | |
| 4.  sedentary | X | | |
| 5.  session | X | | |

**Definition Bank**

A.  to settle down; to grow calm or quiet

B.  official meeting of a court or other formal body

C.  house or dwelling place

D.  performed while seated; not requiring physical exertion

E.  chief official

Name: _____ Date: _____

## Unit I–Lesson 4:
# Base *duc-, duct-*

**Directions:** The words on the chart have the base *duc-, duct-*, which means "lead." Write the letter from the Definition Bank for the correct word.

| Word | Prefix Means | Base Means | Definition |
|------|-------------|-----------|-----------|
| 1. reduce | *re-* = back, again | | |
| 2. educate | *e-* = out, out of | | |
| 3. conductor | *con-* = with, together | | |
| 4. inductee | *in-* = in, on, into | | |
| 5. productive | *pro-* = forth, forward, ahead | | |

**Definition Bank**

A. to teach or train

B. fertile, creative; something that yields results

C. a person brought into military service or other group

D. to make smaller

E. the person in charge of a train or an orchestra

Name: _____  Date: _____

## Unit I–Lesson 5:
# Suffixes -cracy and -crat

**Directions:** The words on the chart have the suffixes *-cracy*, "rule by," or *-crat*, "ruler" or "one who believes in rule by." Write the letter from the Definition Bank for the correct word.

| Word | Base Means | Suffix Means | Definition |
|---|---|---|---|
| 1. democracy | *dem(o)-* = the people | | |
| 2. aristocracy | *artist(o)-* = the best | | |
| 3. plutocrat | *plut(o)-* = wealth | | |
| 4. autocrat | *auto-* = self | | |
| 5. theocracy | *the(o)-* = God | | |

**Definition Bank**

A. a dictator or tyrant who sets his or her own rules

B. one who believes that the rich should govern

C. government of, by, and for the people

D. government by divine laws and commandments

E. government by landowners and the nobility

Name: _____ Date: _____

## Unit II–Lesson 1:
# Base center-, centr(i)-

**Directions:** The words on the chart have the base *center-, centr(i)-*, which means "center." Write the letter from the Definition Bank for the correct word.

| Word | Prefix Means | Base Means | Definition |
|---|---|---|---|
| 1. geocentric | *geo(o)-* = earth | | |
| 2. heliocentric | *heli(o)-* = sun | | |
| 3. hypocenter | *hypo-* = under, below | | |
| 4. concentric | *con-* = with, together | | |
| 5. epicenter | *epi-* = upon | | |

**Definition Bank**

A. orbiting around the sun

B. point on Earth's surface directly above the center of an earthquake

C. point below Earth's surface at which an earthquake originates

D. orbiting around the Earth

E. sharing a common center

Name: _____ Date: _____

## Unit II–Lesson 2:
# Base *audi-, audit-*

**Directions:** The words on the chart have the base *audi-, audit-*, which means "hear" or "listen." Write the letter from the Definition Bank for the correct word. **Hint:** One suffix means "able to be." One suffix makes its word a noun (a thing or idea). The third suffix means "of or relating to."

| Word | Base Means | Suffix Means | Definition |
|---|---|---|---|
| 1. audible | | | |
| 2. audiophile | | *phil-* = love | |
| 3. audiometer | | *meter-* = measure | |
| 4. audition | | | |
| 5. auditory | | | |

**Definition Bank**

A. a tryout or hearing for a role in a performance

B. one who loves listening to music

C. capable of being heard

D. a device that measures hearing

E. pertaining to hearing

Name: _____   Date: _____

## Unit II–Lesson 3:
# Base pon-, pos-, posit-

**Directions:** The words on the chart have the base *pon-, pos-, posit-,* which means "put" or "place." Write the letter from the Definition Bank for the correct word.

| Word | Prefix Means | Base Means | Definition |
|---|---|---|---|
| 1. compost | *com-* = with, together | | |
| 2. deposit | *de-* = down, off | | |
| 3. expose | *ex-* = out | | |
| 4. opponent | *op-, (ob-)* = up against | | |
| 5. composite | *com-* = with, together | | |

**Definition Bank**

**A.** a collection of yard trimmings and other organic materials

**B.** a rival or challenger; one who resists

**C.** synthetic; put together from different parts or substances

**D.** to put in harm's way; to put out in the open

**E.** a substance that settles at the bottom; also, to place something (such as money) for safe keeping

Name: _____    Date: _____

# Unit II–Lesson 4:
# Bases *aqua-* and *hydr(o)-*

**Directions:** The words on the chart have the bases *aqua-* or *hydr(o)-*, which mean "water." (*X* means the word has no prefix.) Write the letter from the Definition Bank for the correct word.

| Word | Prefix/First Base Means | Base Means | Definition |
|---|---|---|---|
| 1. aqueous | X | | |
| 2. hydroplane | | *-plane* = wander | |
| 3. hydrophobia | | *-phobia* = fear of | |
| 4. aquatic | | *-tic* = pertaining to | |
| 5. hydrogen | | *-gen* = produce, give birth | |

**Definition Bank**

A. performed in water, thriving in water

B. rabies; fear of water

C. consisting of water; water-based

D. an element essential to the generation of water

E. to skid over a watery surface

Name: _____ Date: _____

## Unit II–Lesson 5:
# Bases dent- and odont-

**Directions:** The words on the chart have the bases *dent-* or *odont-*, which mean "teeth." (*X* means the word has no prefix.) Write the letter from the Definition Bank for the correct word.

| Word | Prefix Means | Base Means | Definition |
|---|---|---|---|
| 1. exodontist | ex(o)- = out | | |
| 2. trident | tri- = three | | |
| 3. periodontist | peri- = around | | |
| 4. orthodontics | orth(o)- = straight | | |
| 5. dentition | X | | |

**Definition Bank**

A. a harpoon or spear with three prongs

B. a specialist in tooth extraction

C. the specialty of straightening teeth and correcting bites

D. the formation and "cutting" of teeth

E. a specialist in diseases of the gums

Name: _____    Date: _____

# Unit III–Lesson 1:
## Prefix *dia-*

......................................................................

**Directions:** The words on the chart have the prefix *dia-*, which means "through," "across," or "thorough." Write the letter from the Definition Bank for the correct word.

| Word | Prefix Means | Base Means | Definition |
|---|---|---|---|
| **1.** diameter | | *meter-* = measure | |
| **2.** diagnosis | | *gnos-* = know, read | |
| **3.** diagram | | *gram-* = write, draw | |
| **4.** diagonal | | *gon-* = corner, angle | |
| **5.** dialogue | | *log-* = word, speech | |

**Definition Bank**

**A.** thorough explanation of a disease or other problem

**B.** a conversation between two or more people

**C.** a line connecting opposite angles of a polygon

**D.** the length of a straight line through the center of a circle

**E.** a line drawing

Name: _____ Date: _____

## Unit III–Lesson 2:
# Prefixes *peri-*, *circum-*, and *circu-*

**Directions:** The words on the chart have the prefixes *peri-*, *circum-*, or *circu-*, which mean "around." Write the letter from the Definition Bank for the correct word.

| Word | Prefix Means | Base Means | Definition |
|------|--------------|------------|------------|
| **1.** perimeter | | *meter-* = measure | |
| **2.** circumference | | *fer-* = bear, go | |
| **3.** circuitous | | *it-* = go | |
| **4.** periscope | | *scop-* = look, watch | |
| **5.** circumnavigate | | *navig-* = sail | |

**Definition Bank**

**A.** the measure around a circle

**B.** the measure around a polygon

**C.** to sail around a land mass; to sail around the globe

**D.** a device that allows looking around in different directions

**E.** indirect; following a roundabout path

Name: _____    Date: _____

## Unit III–Lesson 3:
# Bases tempor- and chron(o)-

**Directions:** The words on the chart have the bases *tempor-* or *chron(o)-*, which mean "time." (*X* means the word has no prefix.) Write the letter from the Definition Bank for the correct word.

| Word | Prefix Means | Base Means | Definition |
|---|---|---|---|
| 1. contemporary | *con-* = with, together | | |
| 2. chronic | X | | |
| 3. temporary | X | | |
| 4. synchronize | *syn-* = with, together | | |
| 5. chronicles | X | | |

**Definition Bank**

A. persistent; lasting or occurring all the time

B. to set watches at the same time; to arrange at the same time

C. historical records

D. modern; belonging to the same time; of the same age or time period

E. lasting for a limited time; not permanent

Name: _____ Date: _____

## Unit III–Lesson 4:
# Base *later*-

· · · · · · · · · · · · · · · · · · · · · · · · · · · · · · · · · · · · · · · · · · · · · · · · · · · ·

**Directions:** The words on the chart have the base *later*-, which means "side." (*X* means the word has no prefix.) Write the letter from the Definition Bank for the correct word.

| Word | Prefix Means | Base Means | Definition |
|---|---|---|---|
| 1. equilateral | *equi-* = equal | | |
| 2. trilateral | *tri-* = three | | |
| 3. quadrilateral | *quadri-* = four | | |
| 4. lateral | X | | |
| 5. unilateral | *uni-* = one | | |

**Definition Bank**

   A.  one-sided; expressing the opinion of only one person or party

   B.  four-sided; quadrangular

   C.  three-sided; triangular

   D.  having sides of equal length

   E.  sideways; thrown to the side

Name: _____    Date: _____

## Unit III–Lesson 5:

# Base stru-, struct-

**Directions:** The words on the chart have the base *stru-, struct-*, which means "build." (*X* means the word has no prefix.) Write the letter from the Definition Bank for the correct word.

| Word | Prefix Means | Base Means | Definition |
|------|-------------|------------|------------|
| 1. infrastructure | *infra-* = beneath, below, within | | |
| 2. construct | *con-* = with, together | | |
| 3. superstructure | *super-* = over, above | | |
| 4. structure | X | | |
| 5. destructive | *de-* = down, off | | |

**Definition Bank**

A. the underlying support system of a building, bridge, or road

B. causing damage; harmful

C. the part of a building above the foundation

D. to build

E. a building

# Answer Key

## Unit I—Social Studies

**Lesson 1: Directional Prefix *a-*, *ab-*, *abs-*** (page 132)

1. E
2. A
3. C
4. D
5. B

**Lesson 2: Directional Prefix *ad-*** (page 133)

1. C
2. A
3. E
4. D
5. B

**Lesson 3: Base *sed-*, *sid-*, *sess-*** (page 134)

1. C
2. E
3. A
4. D
5. B

**Lesson 4: Base *duc-*, *duct-*** (page 135)

1. D
2. A
3. E
4. C
5. B

**Lesson 5: Suffixes *-cracy* and *-crat*** (page 136)

1. C
2. E
3. B
4. A
5. D

## Unit II—Science

**Lesson 1: Base *center-*, *centr(i)-*** (page 137)

1. D
2. A
3. C
4. E
5. B

**Lesson 2: Base *audi-*, *audit-*** (page 138)

1. C
2. B
3. D
4. A
5. E

**Lesson 3: Base *pon-*, *pos-*, *posit-*** (page 139)

1. A
2. E
3. D
4. B
5. C

**Lesson 4: Bases *aqua-* and *hydr(o)-*** (page 140)

1. C
2. E
3. B
4. A
5. D

**Lesson 5: Bases *dent-* and *odont-*** (page 141)

1. B
2. A
3. E
4. C
5. D

# Answer Key (cont.)

## Unit III—Mathematics

### Lesson 1: Prefix *dia-* (page 142)

1. D
2. A
3. E
4. C
5. B

### Lesson 2: Prefixes *peri-*, *circum-*, and *circu-* (page 143)

1. B
2. A
3. E
4. D
5. C

### Lesson 3: Bases *tempor-* and *chron(o)-* (page 144)

1. D
2. A
3. E
4. B
5. C

### Lesson 4: Base *later-* (page 145)

1. D
2. C
3. B
4. E
5. A

### Lesson 5: Base *stru-*, *struct-* (page 146)

1. A
2. D
3. C
4. E
5. B

# Sample Content-Area Words

## a-, ab-, abs- = "away," "from"

| | | |
|---|---|---|
| abandon | abhorrent | abscond |
| abate | abject | absent |
| abatement | abolish | absolve |
| abdicate | abort | absorb |
| abduct | abrade | abstain |
| aberrant | abrasion | abstention |
| aberration | abrogate | abstract |
| abeyance | abrupt | abuse |

## ad- = "to," "toward," "add to"

| | | | |
|---|---|---|---|
| adaptive | address | adjunct | advantage |
| adapt | adduce | admire | adventure |
| add | adhere | admiration | adventurer |
| addition | adhesive | admission | adventuresome |
| additional | adhesion | admit | adverb |
| addendum | adherence | admittedly | adverse |
| addict | adjacent | admonition | advertise |
| addiction | adjective | adorn | advertisement |
| additive | adjoin | advance | advice |
| add | | advancement | |
| addition | | | |

# Sample Content-Area Words (cont.)

## sed-, sid-, sess- = "sit," "settle"

| | | | |
|---|---|---|---|
| **assess** | **possess** | **reside** | **sedentary** |
| assessor | possession | resided | |
| assessment | possessed | residing | **sediment** |
| assessing | possessing | residence | sedimentary |
| assessed | | residual | |
| | **preside** | residue | **session** |
| **assiduous** | presiding | | |
| | presided | **sedate** | **subside** |
| | president | sedation | |
| | presidency | sedative | **supersede** |

## duc-, duct- = "lead"

| | | | |
|---|---|---|---|
| **abduct** | **deduce** | **introduce** | **reduction** |
| abduction | | introduction | reduce |
| abductor | **duchess** | | |
| | duke | **misconduct** | **seduce** |
| **aqueduct** | | | seduction |
| | **educate** | **product** | |
| **conduct** | educator | produce | **viaduct** |
| conduction | education | producer | |
| conductor | | production | |
| conducive | **induce** | productive | |
| | | unproductive | |
| **deduct** | **induct** | | |
| deduction | induction | | |
| | inductive | | |

# Sample Content-Area Words (cont.)

## -cracy = "rule by"; -crat = "ruler" or "one who believes in rule by"

| | | |
|---|---|---|
| **androcracy** | **bureaucracy** | **plutocracy** |
| **aristocracy** | bureaucrat | plutocrat |
| aristocrat | **democracy** | **technocracy** |
| aristocratic | democrat | technocrat |
| **autocracy** | **gerontocracy** | **theocracy** |
| autocrat | **gynocracy** | theocrat |
| autocratic | gynecocracy | |

## center-, centr(i)- = "center"

| | | |
|---|---|---|
| **amniocentesis** | **centrifuge** | **eccentric** |
| **anthropocentric** | centrifugal | eccentricity |
| anthropocentrism | centrifugation | **egocentric** |
| **central** | **centripetal** | egocentricity |
| **centric** | **concentrate** | **epicenter** |
| **centrist** | concentration | **geocentric** |
| | **concentric** | **heliocentric** |
| | | **hypocenter** |

# Sample Content-Area Words (cont.)

## audi-, audit- = "hear," "listen"

| | | |
|---|---|---|
| audible | audiometer | audition |
| audience | audiotape | auditorium |
| audio-lingual | audiovisual | auditory |
| audiology | audit | inaudible |
| audiologist | auditor | |

## pon-, pos-, posit- = "put," "place"

| | | | |
|---|---|---|---|
| component | dispose | pose | repose |
| | disposition | | |
| compose | | posit | repository |
| composition | expose | | |
| | exposition | position | superimpose |
| composite | | | |
| | impose | positive | suppose |
| compost | imposition | | supposition |
| | | postpone | |
| depose | juxtapose | | transpose |
| | juxtaposition | posture | transposition |
| deposit | | | |
| | oppose | propose | |
| | opposition | proposition | |

# Sample Content-Area Words (cont.)

## aqua-, hydr(o)- = "water"

| | | | |
|---|---|---|---|
| aqua | aquifer | hydrant | hydrous |
| aquaculture | aquiferous | hydrate | hydrolysis |
| aquatic | Aquarius | hydraulic | hydrophilic |
| aqueous | aqualung | hydrochloric | hydrophobic |
| aqueous humor | aquamarine | hydroelectricity | hydrophobia |
| aqueduct | anhydrous | hydrogen | hydroponics |
| aquarium | carbohydrates | hydrogenizes | hydrosphere |
| | dehydrate | hydrogenate | rehydrate |
| | | hydrogenated | |

## dent-, odont- = "tooth," "teeth"

| | | | |
|---|---|---|---|
| dental | dentist | indent | orthodontist |
| dentate | dentistry | indentured | orthodonture |
| dentifrice | dentition | endodontist | pedodontist |
| dentine | dentoid | exodontist | trident |
| dentin | denture | indent | |
| | | indenture | |

# Sample Content-Area Words (cont.)

## dia- = "through," "across," "thorough"

| | | |
|---|---|---|
| **diabetes**<br>diabetic | **dialect** | **diaphanous** |
| **diacritical** | **dialogue** | **diaphragm** |
| **diagonal** | **diagnose** | **diarrhea** |
| **diagram** | **diameter**<br>diametrically | **diatom** |
| | | **diatribe** |

## peri-, circum-, circu- = "around"

| | | |
|---|---|---|
| **circuit**<br>circuitous | **circumpolar** | **perihelion** |
| **circle** | **circumscribe** | **perimeter** |
| **circular** | **circumspect** | **period** |
| **circulate** | **circumstance**<br>circumstantial | **periodical** |
| **circumduct** | **circumvent**<br>circumvention | **periodontics**<br>periodontist |
| **circumference** | **semicircle** | **periphery** |
| **circumnavigate** | **pericardium** | **periscope** |
| | **perigee** | |

# Sample Content-Area Words (cont.)

## tempor-, chron(o)- = "time"

**anachronism**
anachronistic

**chronic**

**chronicle**

**chronology**
chronological

**chronometer**
chronometry

**chronograph**

**chronoscope**

**synchronous**
synchronize
asynchronous
unsynchronized

**contemporary**

**extemporaneous**

**extemporary**

**extemporize**

**tempo**

**temporal**

**temporary**
temporarily

**spatiotemporal**

## later- = "side"

**bilateral**

**collateral**

**equilateral**

**lateral**

**multilateral**

**quadrilateral**

**trilateral**

**unilateral**

# Sample Content-Area Words *(cont.)*

## stru-, struct- = "build"

| | | |
|---|---|---|
| **construct** | **destruct** | **obstruct** |
| constructive | destructive | obstructed |
| construction | destruction | unobstructed |
| **construe** | **infrastructure** | **reconstruct** |
| | | reconstruction |
| **deconstruct** | **instruct** | **restructure** |
| deconstruction | instruction | |
| | instructor | **structure** |
| | instructive | |
| **misconstrue** | | |
| misconstrued | | |

# Flashcards

# a-, ab-, and abs-

# ad-

# Flashcards (cont.)

## "away," "from"

## "to," "toward," "add to"

## Flashcards (cont.)

# *sed-, sid-, and sess-*

# *duc- and duct-*

## Flashcards (cont.)

# "sit," "settle"

# "lead"

## Flashcards (cont.)

# -cracy and -crat

# center- and centr(i)-

# Flashcards (cont.)

## "rule by," "ruler"

## "center"

## Flashcards *(cont.)*

# *audi-* and *audit-*

# *pon-, pos-, and posit-*

# Flashcards (cont.)

# "hear," "listen"

# "put," "place"

## Flashcards *(cont.)*

# *aqua-* and hydr(o)-

# *dent-* and *odont-*

# Flashcards *(cont.)*

"water"

"tooth,"
"teeth"

## Flashcards *(cont.)*

**dia-**

**peri-, circum-, and circu-**

# Flashcards (cont.)

# "through," "across," "thorough"

# "around"

#50865—*Getting to the Roots of Content-Area Vocabulary*

## Flashcards *(cont.)*

# *tempor-* and *chron(o)-*

# *later-*

# Flashcards (cont.)

# "time"

# "side"

## Flashcards (cont.)

# *stru-* and *struct-*

## Flashcards *(cont.)*

# "build"

# Contents of the Digital Resource CD

| Activity Sheets | | |
|---|---|---|
| **Page** | **Activity Sheet** | **Filename** |
| 22–23 | About the Root: Directional Prefix a-, ab-, abs- | abrprefixaababs.pdf |
| 24 | Divide and Conquer: Directional Prefix a-, ab-, abs- | dcprefixaababs.pdf |
| 25 | Making Connections: Word Fun | wordfun.pdf |
| 28–29 | About the Root: Directional Prefix ad- | abrprefixad.pdf |
| 30 | Divide and Conquer: Directional Prefix ad- | dcprefixad.pdf |
| 31 | Making Connections: Word Sort | wordsort.pdf |
| 34–35 | About the Root: Base sed-, sid-, sess- | abrbasesedsidsess.pdf |
| 36 | Divide and Conquer: Base sed-, sid-, sess- | dcbasesedsidsess.pdf |
| 37 | Making Connections: Magic Square | sedsidsessmagicsquare.pdf |
| 40–41 | About the Root: Base duc-, duct- | abrbaseducduct.pdf |
| 42 | Divide and Conquer: Base duc-, duct- | dcbaseducduct.pdf |
| 43 | Making Connections: Authors and Illustrators | authorsandillustrators.pdf |
| 46–47 | About the Root: Suffixes -cracy and -crat | abrsuffixescracycrat.pdf |
| 48 | Divide and Conquer: Suffixes -cracy and -crat | dcsuffixescracycrat.pdf |
| 49 | Making Connections: -cracy and -crat Word Sort | cracycratwordsort.pdf |
| 50–51 | Unit I Review | unitlreview.pdf |
| 54–55 | About the Root: Base center-, centr(i)- | abrbasecentercentri.pdf |
| 56 | Divide and Conquer: Base center-, centr(i)- | dcbasecentercentri.pdf |
| 57 | Making Connections: Magic Square | centercentrimagicsquare.pdf |
| 60–61 | About the Root: Bases audi-, audit- | abrbasesaudiaudit.pdf |
| 62 | Divide and Conquer: Bases audi-, audit- | dcbasesaudiaudit.pdf |
| 63 | Making Connections: Scramble | audiauditscramble.pdf |
| 66–67 | About the Root: Base pon-, pos-, posit- | abrbaseponposposit.pdf |
| 68 | Divide and Conquer: Base pon-, pos-, posit- | dcbaseponposposit.pdf |
| 69 | Making Connections: Guess the Word | guesstheword.pdf |
| 72–73 | About the Root: Bases aqua- and hydr(o)- | abrbasesaquahydro.pdf |
| 74 | Divide and Conquer: Bases aqua- and hydr(o)- | dcbasesaquahydro.pdf |
| 75 | Making Connections: Drawing and Acting | drawingandacting.pdf |
| 78–79 | About the Root: Bases dent- and odont- | abrbasesdentodont.pdf |
| 80 | Divide and Conquer: Bases dent- and odont- | dcbasesdentodont.pdf |
| 81 | Making Connections: Word Sort | dentodontwordsort.pdf |
| 82–83 | Unit II Review | unitllreview.pdf |
| 86–87 | About the Root: Prefix dia- | abrprefixdia.pdf |
| 88 | Divide and Conquer: Prefix dia- | dcprefixdia.pdf |

# Contents of the Digital Resource CD (cont.)

| Activity Sheets | | |
|---|---|---|
| **Page** | **Activity Sheet** | **Filename** |
| 89 | Making Connections: Sketch to Stretch | sketchtostretch.pdf |
| 92–93 | About the Root: Prefixes *peri-*, *circum-*, and *circu-* | abrprefixespericircumcircu.pdf |
| 94 | Divide and Conquer: Prefixes *peri-*, *circum-*, and *circu-* | dcprefixespericircumcircu.pdf |
| 95 | Making Connections: Scramble | pericircumcircuscramble.pdf |
| 98–99 | About the Root: Bases *tempor-* and *chron(o)-* | abrbasestemporchron.pdf |
| 100 | Divide and Conquer: Bases *tempor-* and *chron(o)-* | dcbasestemporchron.pdf |
| 101 | Making Connections: Wordless Skits | wordlessskits.pdf |
| 104–105 | About the Root: Base *later-* | abrbaselater.pdf |
| 106 | Divide and Conquer: Base *later-* | dcbaselater.pdf |
| 107 | Making Connections: Write and Sketch | writeandsketch.pdf |
| 110–111 | About the Root: Base *stru-*, *struct-* | abrbasestrustrcut.pdf |
| 112 | Divide and Conquer: Base *stru-*, *struct-* | dcbasestrustruct.pdf |
| 113 | Making Connections: Word Sort | strustructwordsort.pdf |
| 114–115 | Unit III Review | unitIIIreview.pdf |

| Additional Resources | | |
|---|---|---|
| **Page** | **Additional Resource** | **Filename** |
| 17 | Standards Chart | standards.pdf |
| 129 | 4 x 4 Wordo Matrix | 4x4wordomatrix.pdf |
| 130 | 5 x 5 Wordo Matrix | 5x5wordomatrix.pdf |
| 131 | Word Spokes Chart | wordspokeschart.pdf |
| 132–148 | Additional Assessment Activities | additionalassessments.pdf |
| 149–156 | Sample Content-Area Words | samplewordlists.pdf |
| 157–172 | Flashcards | flashcards.pdf |

# Notes

# Notes